Cindi Wood really knows how to relate to all women, no matter what stage of life they're in. This book was inspiring, heartfelt, and humorous; making me cry, laugh, and pray throughout. In a world that is so hectic, and we do feel "out of control," there is hope in our Almighty God. Cindi lays it all out for anyone to understand and to make a change. I believe anyone that reads this book will walk away with a "changed" attitude in how they look at themselves . . . I know I did.

—Denise Bridges, stay-at-home mom, Georgia

I don't have to be in control because God is! We all need Cindi's reminder to rest in the security of His presence . . . rather than the security of our plans!

—Amy Ross, teacher, South Carolina

Cindi's book was a much needed reminder of how I should/could be living my life, not *without* stress or with freedom from *ever* being frazzled (because that comes with the "job" of being female, wife, and mom), but how to *survive* being frazzled and live victoriously through Christ. This book is all about victorious living for those who choose to spend time with him.

Finding time in our busy schedules to do this is often difficult, but Cindi offers practical, doable advice on finding that "Sacred Balance" and working with "God's Time-Management Plan." Spending time with him allows me to grow to be more like him and respond to the stresses of life in a Christlike manner. This in turn brings glory to God and thus attracts the world around me to Christ.

—Julia Burke, working mom, California

Cindi has, once again, captured the thoughts and experiences of the "frazzled" woman's everyday life. Each chapter of *Too Blessed for This Mess* serves as a tool in our walk with the Lord. Good writing, Cindi!

—Karen Bieber-Guillory, designer, Louisiana

Cindi offers freedom for the frazzled female and strength for the stressed in her new book, *Too Blessed for This Mess*. Her warmth, humor, life experiences, and love for the Lord urge us to grab hold of God's power in the hassles of life, whether in a crisis or in the "diddly-squat" of the every day. I recommend this book for any woman who has ever had a fleeting (or nagging) thought to pack her bags and leave her To-Do list behind!

—Suzanne Orr, homeschooling mom, Texas

What a joy it is to read such significant spiritual insights written in a manner so easy to understand! In her practical, lighthearted style, Cindi communicates so many lessons that I need to hear. She reminds me that allowing the Lord total access to my life is a privilege that restores order to my hectic world. Thanks, Cindi, for making eternal truths so "daily" for me!

—Dianne Alexander, accountant, North Carolina

Cindi Wood has done it again! This book is a "booster shot" of God's word to our thirsty souls. I used it as a daily devotional to enhance my walk with the Lord and to remember his promises. Cindi reminds us that those who have Christ in their lives have the very presence of God living within them to guide us and help us make wise choices. For those who are seeking, she shares the gospel of salvation, boldly and truthfully. Thank you, Cindi, for sharing your heart with us!

—Ann Marie North, empty nester, Florida

I like this book because it truly reflects one who walks the walk and talks the talk. It's about a woman with a mission—reaching out to other women in need. It reminds me that we're all still growing as sisters in Christ, that Jesus is there for us 24-7, which is so easily forgotten in this fast-paced world, and that another's insight is truly what we need, sometimes, to get back on track. It has the component of compassion for others, as Jesus has for us. It gives good examples that women of all ages and stages and walks of life can relate to. It gives guidance and redirection that we all need at some times in our lives. I liked the symbolism of the black ring and the Ebenezer stones as reminders of our struggles and our blessings.

Cindi has done a good job of sharing her innermost feelings, baring her soul in order to help other women. It reminds us that the Holy Spirit nudges and equips us to help others in need, if we will only heed the call to service. This is truly a testimonial of what God will do for us and through us if we invite him into our lives daily! This is a book about an ordinary woman with an extraordinary Savior; a book about one woman using her talent to reach others by story (example) and through Scripture. What a blessing!

—Jo Anne Copeland, nurse, Virginia

Too Blessed
for This Mess

Too Blessed for This Mess

The Frazzled Female's Guide to Overcoming Stress

Cindi Wood

B&H
PUBLISHING GROUP

ISBN: 978-0-8054-4632-6

Published by B&H Publishing Group,
Nashville, Tennessee

Dewey Decimal Classification: 155.9
Subject Heading: STRESS (PSYCHOLOGY) \
WOMEN

1 2 3 4 5 6 7 8 9 10   11 10 09 08 07

A dedication to the life of my grandmother, whose grandchildren affectionately called "Mommy." For more than ninety-nine years, she lived victoriously and crossed her earthly finish line on April 21. She lived each day of life with a physical and spiritual stamina unequal to anyone I know. It's my prayer that "her story" in chapter twenty-three will inspire you to live life with positive determination and full of celebration. My heart swells with joy and pride that I am her granddaughter.

"Give yourself a big hug, Mommy. You've done a great thing!"

Pearl Moss Horne
(1908–2007)

She fought the good fight. She finished the race.
She kept the faith! (2 Tim. 4:7)

I think I can.
        I think I can.
                I think I can.

No, I can't.
        No, I can't.
                No, I can't.

Through Christ I can.
        Through Christ I can.
                Through Christ I can!

"I am able to do all things *through Him* who strengthens me." (Phil. 4:13, italics added)

Contents

My Brain Needs a Detox!

(An introduction for the frazzled female who wants to become *victoriously frazzled!*)

*L*ife driving you crazy? Is your mind overflowing with things to do, places to go, people to care for, with NO TIME LEFT FOR YOU?! Well take heart, sister, and charge on—there's hope for the journey, and hope's name is JESUS!

This morning (4:30 a.m.) I became acutely aware that the enemy—ol' slewfoot himself—was harassing me with his lies: *You'll never be able to finish this manuscript . . . there's not enough time . . . maybe God doesn't really want you to write it . . . (and here's the best one) you're TOO FRAZZLED*!

All of a sudden in that final lie with frazzledness in it, my goal resurfaced and my spirit leaped with excitement. Of course I'm frazzled. That's why I'm *writing* and *speaking* and *teaching* about the truth of Jesus!

It's not like I'm an anomaly. Neither are you. We're all frazzled. It's the nature of the times in which we live. Life is hectic, and the enemy is taking every opportunity to slam through our circumstances and fill our minds with doubts and discouragement. He's the one dishing out those crushing thoughts and overwhelming your soul with despair.

WELL, THIS GAL'S REFUSING TO FALL FOR HIS LIES!

Yes, once again I'm placing my leash into the hand of my heavenly Father and believing him to lead me on and accomplish any and everything he sees fit to accomplish. And if this li'l frazzled female doesn't get it done, then it will be because it was not in his plan in the first place!

What I love about my early morning eureka experience is that the Lord exposed Satan's lie and plopped me right in the middle of victorious truth. Satan filled my brain with junk, but God gave me a holy detox! In fact, the deceiver even did me a favor (by God's grace). He gave me the opportunity to experience my Father's mercy and care and affirmation for what he's calling me to do.

I think of Joseph's comment to his brothers when he encountered them years after they'd left him to die in the pit, "You tried to harm me, but God made it turn out for the best" (Gen. 50:20 CEV).

God will always do that. But we must choose to pay attention and appropriate his power in each and every trying situation. You see, the enemy does try to harm each and every believer through the course of each day. But, God can take those false lies and bring you to a new level of victory!

I'm so thrilled that you've picked up this copy of *Too Blessed for This Mess*. My prayer is that you not put it away until you've got a firm grasp of the love of Jesus on your life. When you have Jesus, you have *who* you need to accomplish anything you need to do. And by the way, that "anything" includes: cleaning your desk at work, patiently caring for your children (or parents), calmly making it through the grocery store, chalking up a little exercise for the day, and finally—falling asleep at night.

The victorious power of Jesus Christ surges through every moment of every day. There's absolutely nothing that his power does not cover!

Writing in the midst of frazzledness, it's my desire to share victorious truths. There's no reason to go through life in a bundle of nerves when victorious living through Jesus Christ is possible!

Before you being reading, let's pray together. Speak these words from your heart and know that your heavenly Father who cares about every detail of your life, hears you as you pray.

> *Dear Father, as I read the message of this book, please open my mind and heart to your truth. I can't do everything and I can't be everywhere. I desire to walk in peace, joy, and victory. Please transform my life into the image of your dear son, and my Lord Jesus. Thank you for loving me and for the victory that is mine through Jesus Christ. I love you.*

Now thank God and believe him for answering your prayers. Know that I'm praying for you too, and together we'll detox in Jesus in the morning, afternoon, evening . . . and all the moments in between.

Cindi Wood

> *"Therefore we do not give up; even though our outer person is being destroyed, our inner person is being renewed day by day. For our momentary light affliction is producing for us an absolutely incomparable eternal weight of glory."* (2 Cor. 4:16–17)

PART ONE

Frazzle-Friendly!

He who dwells in the secret place of the
Most High shall remain stable and fixed under
the shadow of the Almighty.

Psalm 91:1 AMP

'm noticing the phrase *user-friendly* everywhere. I see
it on the packaging of the latest electronic gadgets, as
well as recipes on the Internet. The term reminds me of
the call from the circus barker—persuading people to
enter the circus and enjoy the many attractions there. Even
though I may feel challenged in a particular area, I'm often
persuaded to attack that challenge head-on, simply because
"user friendly" gives me hope that I can pull it off (and
maybe even enjoy the ride!).

Well let me tell you something, girlfriend: you—yes
YOU—have a frazzle-friendly God! He's all about entering
into your stressful life and bringing relief, comfort, and joy
to your most chaotic days. He cares, and furthermore, he

understands all about your stressed-out chemistry and your shredded nerves. He longs for you to turn to him all during the moments of your day. He wants to be a part of the calm moments, as well as those less-than-peaceful ones that rock your world.

The critical role you play in this divine partnership is becoming a *chooser*. God is inviting you into the most glorious, exciting, and dynamic adventure of your life. But you must choose to enter into this love relationship with him. He's near you and he's ready to reveal new facets of his character and new dimensions of his love. These new insights into the heart of God will enable you to face daily living with exhilaration, even on the most trying days.

There were so many years that I lived just short of discovering the power-packed presence of God. You may be like I used to be; you have invited Jesus into your life as your personal Lord and Savior but are relying on your own abilities to navigate through the issues and circumstances of your day.

You don't have to do that anymore. I'm telling you the wonderful and life-changing truth of the matter. You do not have to rely on your own strength to make it through each day.

But in order to make this a reality in your own life, you must choose Jesus. You must first choose him as your personal Lord and Savior, and then you must choose him as your partner moment by moment, day by day. If you have not yet begun this love journey with your Lord, I invite you to turn to "How to Become a Christian" on page 143, to learn how to begin your personal relationship with Jesus Christ.

And then, please don't stop "short of the journey"! Once you've believed the Lord to be faithful to save you from your appointment in hell, then believe him to provide his power moment by moment as life hits you hard.

I'm excited for you to work your way through the pages of *Too Blessed for This Mess*. The truths presented in this little book have been life changing for me. When I finally grasped the reality of who God is and then learned to grab hold of his power in daily circumstances, I literally entered into the spiritual dimension of *Cindi's life here on planet Earth*. It's a whole new love relationship paradigm with Jesus for me!

I certainly don't claim to have mastered all of the life-changing truths that God has to offer me, but I have truly become an eager and expectant student. I just love learning about him, his ways, and how I can appropriate his power in my life.

I'm eager for you to join me and happy that you've chosen to move along in your journey of loving the Lord in a new and intimate way. Together, we'll move forward to explore the power of his love that's available in a deeply intimate personal relationship with Jesus Christ.

- Have you invited Jesus Christ to live in your heart?

- In what particular areas of your life do you need to experience the Lord's victory to make it through?

CHAPTER ONE

Be Still and Let God Fight!

"The LORD will fight for you; you need only to be still."

Exodus 14:14 NIV

I just can't take it anymore! That's what Danita said as she flopped down in the recliner in her den. It was late afternoon, and plenty of evening duties still lay before her. She felt like she'd been putting out fires all day long with no one to help. Somewhere inside she knew she shouldn't be feeling so irritated and helpless. She was running out of energy and not enjoying life the way she used to. She breathed a prayer of *Lord, please help me,* but it was more out of desperation than a sincere cry for help.

Oh, it's so easy to sing the I-can't-take-it-anymore blues! And before you know it, that annoying tune gets trapped in your mind and you can't stop humming it. My friend Debbie says it's like throwing your hands in the air and letting the tide carry you out. When demands are piled high and energy is running low, it's easy to get swallowed up in discouragement and self-pity.

Here's the good news. Your God is strong and mighty to save, and he's waiting and longing to invade your daily circumstances and pull you out of the pit!

> *He lifted me out of the slimy pit, out of the mud and mire; he set my feet on a rock and gave me a firm place to stand.* (Ps. 40:2 NIV)

Only God can bring stability out of the messes of life. He loves for you to call on him when you can't take it anymore. As your heavenly Father, it delights him to comfort you and rescue you. He understands your stress and how the events of daily living can leave you haggard and depleted.

Honestly, there are times when living can take the life out of you, can't it? But if you turn to Jesus and allow him to, he will fight your battles, restore your joy, and usher you into victorious living.

Women are fighting lots of battles these days and that battlefield includes husbands, children, parents, illnesses, finances, housework, all sorts of relationships, the work-place, that never-ending To-Do list, etc. There seem to be more things (and people) to manage with less time to do so. Life is just hectic!

But thanks be to God. He has a plan!

The story of Moses in the fourteenth chapter of Exodus has helped me understand the role of God and the role of me in that divine plan of his—you know, that plan that unfolds right in the middle of the stress of everyday living.

Let's take a look at this account of Moses recorded in the Scriptures.

> *Then the LORD spoke to Moses. "Tell the Israelites to turn back and camp in front of Pi-hahiroth, between Migdol and the sea; you must camp in front of Baal-zephon, facing it by the sea. Pharaoh will say*

of the Israelites: They are wandering around the land in confusion; the wilderness has boxed them in. I will harden Pharaoh's heart so that he will pursue them. Then I will receive glory by means of Pharaoh and all his army, and the Egyptians will know that I am the LORD.*" So the Israelites did this.*

When the king of Egypt was told that the people had fled, Pharaoh and his officials changed their minds about the people and said: "What have we done? We have released Israel from serving us." So he got his chariot ready and took his troops with him; he took 600 of the best chariots . . . of Egypt, with officers in each one. The LORD *hardened the heart of Pharaoh king of Egypt, and he pursued the Israelites, who were going out triumphantly. The Egyptians—all Pharaoh's horses and chariots, his horsemen, and his army—chased after them and caught up with them as they camped by the sea beside Pi-hahiroth, in front of Baal-zephon.*

As Pharaoh approached, the Israelites looked up and saw the Egyptians coming after them. Then the Israelites were terrified and cried out to the LORD *for help. They said to Moses: "Is it because there are no graves in Egypt that you took us to die in the wilderness? What have you done to us by bringing us out of Egypt? Isn't this what we told you in Egypt: Leave us alone so that we may serve the Egyptians? It would have been better for us to serve the Egyptians than to die in the wilderness."*

But Moses said to the people, "Don't be afraid. Stand firm and see the LORD'S *salvation He will provide for you today; for the Egyptians you see today, you will never see again. The* LORD *will fight for you; you must be quiet."* (Exod. 14:1–14)

You see, God's plan did not make sense. In fact, the plans of God often go against common-sense thinking. He actually instructed Moses to turn them away from Canaan, the Promised Land, and lead them toward the Red Sea. This action would lead Pharaoh to think they were confused and just wandering around. God orchestrated this event, you see, to bring glory to himself. As Pharaoh and his army pursued the children of Israel, it appeared that God's chosen people were doomed. The Israelites thought so themselves. Instead of trusting, they cried out to the Lord and complained to Moses, telling him it would have been better for them to serve the Egyptians than die in the desert! But Moses, full of God's vision, encouraged and comforted them with the assurance of God's deliverance.

> *The LORD will fight for you; you need only to be still.* (Exod. 14:14 NIV)

What appeared to be total chaos was not! It was God's plan to bring glory to himself. His children, however, were not faithful in believing that the same God who had always taken care of them would do it again.

I'm just like those children of Israel at times—wandering around and feeling doomed to stress and forgetting that my God is in control and leading me onward to victory! Oh, but I want to get better at trusting him to fight my battles. And the truth is, *I am getting better* at being still and allowing him to take over. And that's something to celebrate each time it happens—my Lord, fighting my battles!

A personal example of *being still* comes to mind that so accurately expresses this concept. As a small child, I escaped to the deep end of the pool one day and jumped into water way over my head. I remember fighting underwater, trying to get back above water. The harder I fought, the deeper I went. I didn't know how to swim to the top. Exhausted, I stopped fighting and expected to drown. Still and helpless, I then floated to the top, where I was spotted and a rescue team quickly pulled me out.

Does this sound like you, in circumstances you are facing? Are you struggling, doing everything imaginable to "fight" whatever battle you're going through only to find yourself feeling exhausted and helpless?

Be still, my friend. Empty your heart of its anguish and toss out your battle-worn emotions. Cease your frantic thoughts and actions of desperation. Stop fighting and ease into the arms of your Savior, who is waiting to rescue you. He's the strong and mighty warrior, and he *will* win the fight!

- What battles are you currently facing?

- Are you willing to be still so that God can fight for you?

CHAPTER TWO

The Secret Place

He who dwells in the secret place of the Most
High shall remain stable and fixed under the
shadow of the Almighty.

Psalms 91:1 AMP

*O*ne day last winter it was raining, and I was stuck
inside on the treadmill. I often use my exercise time
to memorize Scripture. On that particular day I placed
my wrinkled index card with Psalm 91:1 before me. Two
words lodged in my heart. For the next hour, I could not
get "secret place" out of my mind! It seemed to me that
God was romancing my heart with that concept. I became
captivated with the whole notion of the secret place, talking with the Lord about where it was and how to get there.
Meditating on this Scripture led me into deeper intimacy
with my Savior that morning (along with rebooting my
exercise routine!).

I love it when God pulls out his heavenly highlighter
and circles a Scripture verse just for me! He does do that,
you know. He longs to bring each of us deeper into intimacy with him by romancing our hearts and capturing our
attention in unexpected ways. He longs to be involved in

15

a one-on-one relationship with you, with me. More and more I'm experiencing him, delighting my very soul with his tenderness.

Stasi Eldredge speaks of this God-longing in *Captivating*, the book she authored with her husband John.

> The vast desire and capacity a woman has for intimate relationships tells us of God's vast desire and capacity for intimate relationships. In fact, this may be the most important thing we ever learn about God—that he yearns for relationship with us. . . . The whole story of the Bible is a love story between God and his people. He yearns for us. He cares. He has a tender heart.[1]

So. This secret place is the special place shared by you and God. It's emotional, mental, and physical. It may be a place of great joy. It may also be a place of tears. It's a place where you meet your Savior in the crevices of your heart. And all who go there have a different experience. The secret place is reserved for God's children who have invited Jesus Christ to live in their hearts as their personal Lord and Savior. And even then, it's reserved for only the ones who desire it with their whole being. It's the depth of Jesus Christ.

In Jeremiah 29:13, that great prophet tells us that we will find the Lord when we seek him with our whole heart. I'm learning to do that, and with my learning comes a great longing to know him more and more. As I visit this secret place, I long to stay there. It seems that all the words in the world can't describe the joy, peace, and fulfillment I experience being so close to Jesus.

This place of intimacy is not a mysterious place in the sense of having to work your way through a maze to get there, but it is mysterious in that the depth of Jesus is unexplainable and indescribable. I don't mean to make your relationship with Jesus seem magical, but it is supernatural. Paul talks about "secret wisdom" in the books of Corinthians. He tells how believers can understand God's truth because of the Spirit living in them.

> *We have not received the spirit of the world but the Spirit who is from God, that we may understand what God has freely given us.* (1 Cor. 2:12 NIV)

Maybe you've never experienced this kind of depth with Jesus Christ. It's OK! You should not feel guilty but excited with the reality that you can certainly experience a deeper intimacy with him if you want to. It's your choice.

It's an unnatural choice, worldly speaking, because it requires that you get still and quiet before God. Everything in our lives today calls us away from that "quiet and still place." So you'll have to put some determined spiritual muscle behind your choice to know your Lord more intimately. But I can tell you, it's worth the effort! Growing your relationship with Jesus will calm your nerves and refresh your spirit—even in the midst of the daily clamor of life. Truthfully, I don't know how he does that—but I can vouch that he does.

If you're still not quite convinced that you want to invest the time to deepen your love relationship with the Lord, let me serve up some reasons for your consideration, backing each up with Scripture.

- *Stability of life:* "[She] who dwells in the secret place of the Most High shall remain *stable and fixed* under the shadow of the Almighty" (Ps. 91:1 AMP).

- *Peaceful and at rest:* "Come to me, all you who are weary and burdened, and I will give you rest" (Matt. 11:28 NIV).

- *Reflection of Jesus:* "Let your light so shine before men that they may see your moral excellence and your praiseworthy, noble, and good deeds and recognize and honor and praise and glorify your Father Who is in heaven" (Matt. 5:16 AMP).

Convinced yet? How about:

- *Assurance of his nearness:* "Draw near to God, and He will draw near to you" (James 4:8).

- *Steadiness of nerves:* "I am at rest in God alone; my salvation comes from Him. He alone is my rock and my salvation, my stronghold; I will never be shaken" (Ps. 62:1–2).

Hopping onboard for a deeper spiritual journey will require that you make knowing Jesus your top priority. If you want to know him more deeply, you can! And the way you learn about him is to spend time with him. It's simple in theory, but difficult in practice. You must be willing to put aside all and follow him. The world will call you away. Satan will call you away. Your human nature will call you away. You must be determined to be obedient in your love for him and your desire to know him.

I often pray: *Lord, I don't know how to love you with all my heart and all my soul and all my strength. Will you teach me? Give me the desire to love you more!*

It's then that he seems to reach down, take hold of me, and assure me that if my desire is there, our love relationship will certainly grow as I meditate on Scripture and seek his face daily. Furthermore, it doesn't matter if I grow this intimacy quickly or slowly. All that is important is that I'm growing it! The sweetness of taking those baby steps of loving him is more than I can describe.

- Do you want to grow your love for Jesus?

- How will deepening your love for him help you deal with stress?

CHAPTER THREE

Sacred Balance

"No, in all these things we are more than victorious
through Him who loved us."

Romans 8:37

*S*andi loves the Lord, and she loves her family. There's no question about her love. What she does question, however, is how to make it all work—how to do it all, be it all, and experience joy in the middle of it all. She learned a long time ago to put the Lord first in her life, and she feels as if she's done that. She reads her Bible on most days, goes to church every Sunday, and remembers to pray before meals. She knows her family is supposed to come next. She's worked hard on that one! Being very involved with each of her children's schedules, she's the ultimate I'm-here-for-you Mom. She has sacrificed her own pleasures, even her needs, to spend more time with her family. And now—with increasing demands at work and at home—she's exasperated and wondering, *How did my life get so out of balance?*

Truth is, our stress level increases with our effort to do more and be more. With an increased drive to "get it all done," we're paying a high price. And we actually reduce our ability to accomplish tasks efficiently. It gets increasingly difficult to make decisions and takes longer to complete even simple tasks. We get forgetful and easily distracted, along with becoming just plain worn out!

Single or married, children or none, young or old, whatever your status in life may be, you just might be living totally *out of balance*. If so, you're likely feeling restless, maybe hopeless, and possibly defeated because of your circumstances. Rest assured, dear sister, God has something far better in mind for you!

According to Romans 8:37, we are conquerors of our daily schedules—through Jesus Christ! Regardless of the unbalanced mess you may find yourself in, you are ultimately the one in charge of your schedule. If there are areas in your life that need extra attention, you need to back off from doing some lesser important things.

Read aloud each of the following statements. SHOUT them if it makes you feel better!

I cannot do everything.
I cannot be everything to everybody.
I will stop trying to do it all.
I will stop trying to be it all.

(In fact, it may be helpful to jot these down on an index card, pulling it out when you're hit with a weak moment of temptation to take on more than you can handle.)

Listen up, megawoman!

You were never meant to handle everybody's problems and take care of every situation that unfolds before you. It's unhealthy to even try. Women everywhere are juggling too many roles and finding insufficient time to do all the things they are trying to do. Packing each hour as full as you can leaves you more stressed than ever before.

So, having said all of the above, is the problem that there's not enough time or that you are trying to do too much? "Sacred balance" is living in a place where you learn to evaluate your time by God's design and according to his plan. Consulting with him is the only way to achieve balance in daily living.

At the time of this writing, I'm a caregiver for my dad and my grandmom. I love them and love to take care of them. I know it's a gift/responsibility from God that I do so. There are some weeks, however, that I don't feel like I give them adequate attention. Obviously I can't spend all my time with them, and God doesn't want me to. Only he can instruct me how to balance my time with them with the other things he is calling me to do.

How do I receive that instruction? By spending time with Jesus, meditating on Scripture, and seeking his counsel. There are times he also impresses me to seek the counsel of wise and godly friends and family.

I don't take the invitation of Jeremiah 33:3 lightly. I'm training myself to continually seek the Lord, asking his opinion, and expecting him to lead me through his Word, his circumstances, and his people.

> *Call to Me and I will answer you and tell*
> *you great and wondrous things you do not know.*
> (Jer. 33:3)

Getting to know Jesus more intimately, and pursuing a lifestyle of talking over the details of everyday with him gives you a new and different perspective on what's truly important in life. The Holy Spirit will counsel you (that's his job) as you seek answers from him about your daily schedule.

> *And I will ask the Father, and He will give you*
> *another Counselor to be with you forever.*
> (John 14:16)

According to Romans 8:34, "Jesus also is at the right hand of God and intercedes for us."

Oh my. Just imagine it. Jesus is sitting at the right hand of God and interceding for YOU! He's praying for you to have a life that is balanced, healthy, and joyful.

I must confess to you that because this reality is so exciting to me, I'm a bit frustrated because I know it's impossible to cover all the aspects of moving into a balanced life during these few pages, but I do realize—I don't have to cover it!

God himself is speaking to you! Hear him? Are you listening?

If you believe and heed his instruction, he will help restore the joy of your salvation and lead you along the road to balanced living. Oh, I'm praying you will listen and move with obedience in the direction he's leading you.

Being one with Jesus will give you new vision and keep you absolutely fresh for everything he wants you to be doing. You'll be more than empowered through the never-ending supply of the life of God!

- In what areas do you need the sacred balance of Jesus in your life?

- Are you willing to spend time with him, meditate on Scripture, and seek his counsel in order to achieve it?

CHAPTER FOUR

God's Time-Management Plan

"Bring the full 10 percent into the storehouse so that there may be food in My house. Test Me in this way," says the LORD of Hosts. "See if I will not open the floodgates of heaven and pour out a blessing for you without measure."

Malachi 3:10

The year was 1990. Once again I prayed, *Lord, if you'll help me, I will begin each morning with you. I love you and I want to be with you.* My prayer was sincere and my motive pure. I truly wanted to be with Jesus! So, with my plan in place and my Bible and journal by my side, I got up at 4:30 the following morning. I decided that it was 4:30 or nothing. We were out the door by 6:30 headed for the baby-sitter for Lane, elementary school for Brandon, and work for me at the local middle school where I taught. Good plan, but the same thing happened each morning as I—full of resolve—got up and positioned myself in our den with my Bible in my lap: I fell asleep!

Oh how Satan rushed in trying to defeat me and make me feel worthless. *Why don't you wait until your children get older? Then it will be easier to have this quiet time with the Lord.* That was the thought he planted. He also poured on the guilt.

I'll never forget the way I experienced God's love at that time of my life. Instead of being consumed with the negatives, I sensed his loving voice saying, *Thank you for coming!*

See, my heavenly Father knew all about my tired body and the many demands placed on me from being a wife, mother, and teacher. He understands all about you, too, and that it may not be the easiest thing you do, to come to that quiet place with him. I believe with all my heart that the Lord honors a commitment made from a heart that's filled with love for him. He is so glad that you long to spend some time in his presence, and he will bless you for showing up!

I came to a new understanding some years ago while I was preparing a workshop on time management for a conference of Christian women. As I studied and committed this event to the Lord, he placed a Scripture verse in my mind that I had learned as a child: It's the Malachi 3:10 verse that you read earlier. Here's the New International Version translation:

> *Bring the whole tithe into the storehouse, that*
> *there may be food in my house. Test me in this," says*
> *the* LORD *Almighty, "and see if I will not throw open*
> *the floodgates of heaven and pour out so much blessing*
> *that you will not have room enough for it.*

I remember thinking, *Yes, Lord? I'm working on TIME, not TITHE.*

Then he zapped me (I love it when he does that!) with the reality of what he was saying. It was so exciting, I couldn't write it quickly enough.

Yes, this does have to do with tithing, but it also has to do with time!

Dear sister, you may not have a lot of time, but you do have *some* time! And that "some time" is what he's calling you to, even if it's not a lot.

During those years when my children were young and my responsibilities included being a wife, mother, and teacher, I did not have a lot of time each day to spend quietly with my Lord, but I did have some time to go there each and every day.

I can't decide what's the right amount of time for you, just as you don't have a clue what's right for me. It's totally between you and God. It's useless and a waste of energy for you to compare yourself with others in this area too. These sacred moments between you and your Lord are strictly between the two of you! Only the Lord knows the amount of time for worship, Bible study, and prayer that he has in mind for you at this time of your life. This is what makes your relationship with him so unique and personal. And, he will bless you for living in obedience to what he's calling you to do!

As I continued to prepare for that workshop, I learned about a *holy multiplying principle.*

God said to the children of Israel, "Test me in this . . . and see if I will not throw open the floodgates of heaven and pour out so much blessing that you will not have room enough for it."

He's saying the same thing to you and me concerning our time with him! God understands our schedules, and he promises that if we will give him some time—even if we only have a little time—he will take it and multiply our blessings because we are giving to him in love and obedience.

Oh, how I hope that you are beginning to understand how much God loves you and understands you. He's not asking the impossible. He's asking you to love him and spend time getting to know him deeply and intimately. He's wanting you to experience the blessings that will be yours when you make time with him a priority in your life!

How will you be able to decide how much time is the right amount of time? He'll tell you. God will impress upon your heart how much quiet and uninterrupted time he wants you to spend with him. Remember his Holy Spirit will guide you and lead you in this area. The time you spend one on one with him may even vary from day to day and will probably change as the responsibilities of your life change.

Another verse that touched my heart during those preparation days was also a verse from the Old Testament.

> *I'd rather for you to be faithful and to know me than to offer sacrifices.* (Hosea 6:6 CEV)

More than sacrificing time, taking on service projects, and attending meetings for him—he wants me to *know him!* Instead of working for him, he'd rather I grow more intimate with him. He wants me to be *with him* more than he wants me to do things *for him!*

What a revelation I experienced that day . . . one that continues to affect my walk with my Lord!

- Would you agree you have *some* time to spend with Jesus?

- Are you ready to enter into his blessings by obeying his call to this quiet place?

CHAPTER FIVE

Resting in Jesus

He said to them, "Come away by yourselves to
a remote place and rest a while."

Mark 6:31

*T*his e-mail from my friend Gail got my attention:

> *My problems pale in comparison to what oth-*
> *ers are going through. I hesitate to even speak about*
> *them. I feel like they are so trivial—until I freeze and*
> *feel trapped, unable to create any movement in my*
> *life. . . . I know God loves me. I know he wants to use*
> *me. I just don't see how he can.*

Oh, haven't you felt that same way? Even as I write, I've
just been informed of new tragedy and heartache for people
I know. These heartaches include illness, broken dreams,
and even death.

These are BIG things. And when I hear about these
tragedies and major life events that others are suffering
through, I feel that my trials are so insignificant and so . . .
well, NOTHING!

Here's the reality, though. Even though what you are
experiencing at any given moment may not be as horrible

as what others are having to endure, the accumulation of little things can drive you nuts!

Do I hear an amen?

It makes no difference what is driving you to *freeze and feel trapped, unable to create any movement in your life,* but it does matter that you feel that way.

You and I must remember something very significant about the character of our God: If it concerns us, then it's important to him! For some reason we have a difficult time accepting that as reality. But it's totally true. We think our piddly little stresses don't matter to him—or maybe we feel guilty over the fact that we are bothered about them in the first place.

At a recent Frazzled Female Conference, I was speaking about how God wants us to talk with him about anything that bothers us; anything that stresses us and robs us of our joy—ANYTHING! A young mother of three little boys approached me during the break and said, "God doesn't want me to talk to him about the way my boys scatter their dirty underwear through the house."

I retaliated with a laugh (hopefully a convincing one), "Oh yes he does!"

Here's the invitation extended to you by your Lord:

> *Come with me by yourselves to a quiet place and get some rest.* (Mark 6:31 NIV)

You need to rest just as much from everyday living as you need rest and recovery from the major events of life. And the rest you need is found in that quiet place with Jesus Christ.

One morning a couple of years ago, I was sitting at my computer, trying to stay on the task of finishing the manuscript of *Too Blessed for This Mess.* I knew the Lord had called me to it, and I was determined to get it done. But this particular morning I was overwhelmed with life and all the things that lay in my realm of responsibility for that day—and the days ahead. I cried out to the Lord, saying, "Father, I know you want me to write this study for you, but I just can't seem to get it done right now!"

King Jesus did what he has done time and time again. He rushed to show me his love and his encouragement. My Bible was in front of me and had fallen open to Psalm 57:2. Through tears, here's what I read:

> *I will cry to God Most High, Who performs on my behalf and rewards me—Who brings to pass His purposes for me and surely completes them!* (AMP)

I taped that verse to my computer for continual reference as I wrote. Meditating on that Scripture kept me encouraged and focused when the enemy tried to distract my thinking.

It's God's promise that he WILL complete what he has called you to do. You just need to walk in obedience step-by-step until it's done.

It continues to amaze me more and more that God is interested in the diddly-squat things of life (now that's spiritual, huh!) and is concerned over the minutest details. I think that just might astound me more than the fact that he is the God of big things and events. He does care when my life is crippled because of the piling up of little things, such as: *dirty clothes to wash, bills to pay, house to clean, phone calls to make.*

You see, ALL of life is important to him—not just the big things. Knowing this draws me to love him more and more. There's absolutely nothing that he is not concerned with that has to do with me!

Realizing more about the depth of his love concerning the trivial things in my life makes me more determined than ever to embrace my love relationship with him. The greatest goal of my life is to love him. Paul's goal has become mine too:

> *My determined purpose is that I may know*
> *Him—that I may progressively become more deeply*
> *and intimately acquainted with Him, perceiving*
> *and recognizing and understanding the wonders*
> *of His Person more strongly and more clearly.*
> (Phil. 3:10 AMP)

Having experienced his glory and his tremendous love for me through the trials of my life, there's nothing I want more than to know him and love him with everything in me! For me that's the *only* way to find rest in the hassles of everyday living. Plunging into Jesus restores my focus and my sanity. When life crashes in (which it often does), I just pull aside with him to that quiet place and rest for a short while. In growing my intimacy with him on a daily basis, I take baby steps toward my Savior, and those little steps of obedience produce BIG blessings. That's God's arithmetic!

- What "little problems" in your life have you assumed God is not interested in?

- Spend a few moments now, talking with him about those areas.

PART TWO

Control Freaks

Be completely humble and gentle; be patient,
bearing with one another in love.

Ephesians 4:2 NIV

Sporting my baby boomers T-shirt, I share many characteristics with my fellow teammates, one of those being,
I WANT TO BE IN CONTROL!

Yep, I grew up learning to be independent and go after
what I wanted. My mom modeled this lifestyle for her
little boomerette by growing a successful realty company
and going after her contractor's license so she could build
houses. She was all about being in charge and planning for
the future—her way!

I always admired those characteristics in my mom. She
taught me to set goals and be determined about reaching
them; she was a great role model for me as I moved into
young adulthood and gradually began to take control of

those areas in my life that revolved around being a young wife and mother.

The greatest attribute I saw in my mom, however, manifested itself just days before she made her departure to heaven. Up until the moment she made her "divine choice," I was very involved in her recovery fight—meeting with doctors, regularly consulting the hospital staff about her health issues, and finding out everything I could about the programming at Presbyterian Hospital for cancer patients and their families. My mom was a wonderful team player in this effort. She fought to get well, keeping her focus on her family, her building career, even selling houses from her hospital room there in Charlotte, North Carolina.

After years of valiant fighting and modeling a life of faith in her Lord, the earthly battle with cancer ended. The choice she made was one of submitting to the control of Jesus Christ. It was his timing, and she knew it. With the words "I'm ready" came great peace in her heart that shone on her face and transferred to the rest of us who were suffering with her.

Life's all about control—from the moment we're born until the moment we step into our life in heaven. We women—stubborn by nature—naturally take charge on the home front; at the workplace; and in our communities, churches, and surrounding areas in between. God in his perfect workmanship made us that way, and it's a grand thing.

However, this control nature of ours can GET OUT OF CONTROL!

I really think you'll enjoy this "control track" on your victorious living journey. I've been tremendously encouraged as I've written what the Lord has spoken to me throughout these pages. I'm finding that it all comes down to seeking his direction and listening to his voice—more than getting caught up in having to have things done in my way, my timing, and my plan!

And those people I rush to control—well, they belong to my Lord too! I'm realizing it's a wonderful gift of freedom—from me to me—when I place those reins I've attached to them in the very capable hands of my heavenly Father.

As a *control person,* I've become transformed by the grace of Jesus—my family thanks him! When I focus on the Lord, everything about controlling circumstances and people sharpens into focus. The little things remain little, and the things that need my intervention get taken care of in his way, not mine. In the process, I'm exhibiting the love and compassion of Jesus and moving about reflecting him, not me.

I'll rush to say I'm definitely a "work in progress," but I'm celebrating the growth I'm experiencing in this area. More miles to cover, but I'm gathering steam to make it happen with each step I travel.

I like what Oswald Chambers said about the life transformed by God:

> *The greatest characteristic a Christian can exhibit is this completely unveiled openness before God, which allows that person's life to become a mirror for others. When the Spirit fills us, we are transformed and by beholding God we become mirrors. You can always tell when someone has been beholding the glory of the Lord, because your inner spirit senses that he mirrors the Lord's own character.*[2]

So sit tight (with him) as you charge ahead to learn what *you* need to know about *being in control!*

CHAPTER SIX

Controlling Your Circumstances

Trust in the LORD with all your heart,
and do not rely on your own understanding.

Proverbs 3:5

The plane landed at 11:46 a.m. My connecting flight was four terminals away and scheduled to depart at 12:01. Needless to say, I was a bit frantic as we touched down on the runway, visualizing myself sprinting through the airport to board the next leg of my flight. Armed with one big carry-on bag that had to be pried out of the overhead bin and one determined (if not stubborn) spirit, I barreled off that plane and set my gaze toward Gate 4D. Weaving through the crowd and trying not to take anybody out, I felt a nudge in my spirit saying, *You know, you're probably not going to make this one.* I remember a brief feeling of panic with that reality, but almost immediately I was flooded with God's peace. I panted, *Lord, I'm going to try my best to make it to that plane, but if I don't I know you have another plan.*

I have a good handle on those out-of-control feelings. I know them well. Feelings of anxiety, helplessness, determination, and even anger are not foreign to me when I think of those times when circumstances did not go the way I had planned.

Delving into the book of Acts, I find that what happened in Saul's life on that providential road trip to Damascus speaks directly to me about some control issues in my life. He was a man who had his act together, and he was on a mission! Nothing deterred him from breathing those murderous threats and slaughtering countless disciples of the Lord. Nothing, except God himself!

> *Meanwhile Saul, still breathing threats and murder against the disciples of the Lord, went to the high priest and requested letters from him to the synagogues in Damascus, so that if he found any who belonged to the Way, either men or women, he might bring them as prisoners to Jerusalem. As he traveled and was nearing Damascus, a light from heaven suddenly flashed around him. Falling to the ground, he heard a voice saying to him, "Saul, Saul, why are you persecuting Me?"*
>
> *"Who are You, Lord?" he said.*
>
> *"I am Jesus, whom you are persecuting," He replied. "But get up and go into the city, and you will be told what you must do." (Acts 9:1–6)*

Stopped in his tracks by God himself, and in a split second.

I've had that happen before, haven't you? Nothing quite as dramatic as Saul's experience, but there have certainly been times when, without warning or announcement, *my plan* was abruptly halted, and I was forced to go to that proverbial Plan B.

I see this phenomenon most often presenting itself in the form of "interruptions to my schedule." Now truly, a lot of these occurrences are little things in the whole scheme of life. But honestly, don't those little interruptions have a way of driving you berserk?

They're just life things, living in the twenty-first century fast-track things. And I believe that God uses these "little things" to remind me that he is ultimately in control of my schedule and my circumstances.

By nature, I'm an organizer. When I organize, it puts *me* in control of my schedule, my circumstances, my day . . . at least *that's the plan.* So when things don't go according to my organizational system, I get a little miffed. And when things get turned completely upside down (which happens quite a lot lately), I can really get stressed. The bottom line here: I like to be in control!

So what's a control person like me, maybe you, to do?

Give these tendencies to the Lord. Ask him to help you turn to him in ordering the events of your day. Now, that's not to say you don't make lists and you don't plan. It's just a reminder that there will be plenty of times when your plans get annihilated, and you don't have to get carried off with the debris when that happens. YOUR GOD IS IN CONTROL!

He wants you to rest in the security of his presence instead of the security of your plans. Spending time worshipping my Lord and meditating on Scripture is helping me flow in the lifestyle of experiencing the presence of God during the ins and outs of my day. Now, when the unexpected happens (which is to be expected), I'm learning to relax in him and move in his spiritual flow, so to speak. Honestly, most of life is just not worth freaking out over. And besides—freaking out doesn't do one thing to help me regain the control that I lost!

Oh, by the way, I did make that flight—just barely, but that was enough. I had a strong feeling that day that God was using that opportunity to test my willingness to place my trust in him instead of getting unnerved because I was no longer in charge. That whole event, it seems, was not about catching that plane at all. It was about catching what God wanted to teach me:

I don't have to be in control . . . God is!

As I write, I'm celebrating what occurred that day. I passed a *control test* . . . and I have a feeling before I finish these next chapters, there will be one or two more headed my way.

- Are you a "controlling person"?

- Do you need some leveling out in that area?

CHAPTER SEVEN

Trusting God's Control

I am grateful that God always makes it possible
for Christ to lead us to victory.

2 Corinthians 2:14 CEV

*A*ndrea was chairman of the *Walk for Those Who Can't* event for her community. Even though she didn't feel equipped to pull it off, she agreed because she strongly felt God was calling her to head up this project. For months she and her coworkers strategically made their plans. They covered everything from food and sales vending to landscaping around the outdoor track. She felt at peace that everything was under control and everybody was cooperating—except the weatherman! His prediction of rain had her heart racing with panic. She couldn't believe God would let it rain on this particular day. She had faithfully prayed over every committee member and every detail of her plans. It was God, after all, who had called her to do this, and she had agreed because she wanted to be obedient to his calling. Now the beginning of the walk was only hours away, and the forecast for the entire day was rain!

Poor Andrea. I can just imagine her frustration and confusion.

I can think of several times in my life when I knew that I knew God was in control, and his being in control meant that he would carry through to completion the "whatever" I had envisioned. In other words, I thought I knew and understood the perfect will of God in these particular events.

And then, nothing went according to the plans . . . *mine,* not his!

I kind of think that's what Saul meant when he said, "Who are You, Lord?" (Acts 9:5).

I really believe he knew who the Lord was, I think he was just reacting with a who-are-you-and-what-are-you-doing kind of attitude. I have no way of knowing that; I'm just basing it on how I've sometimes reacted to the Lord. When I've committed my plans to him in prayer and I've done my best to carry them through, I just have a hard time believing it when things go wrong!

Are you ever like that? Do you remember times when you were absolutely certain God would not allow something to happen and then the very thing you just knew wouldn't happen, did?

That's when I rely heavily on the truth of Scripture.

> *But thanks be to God, who always leads us in triumphal procession in Christ . . .* (2 Cor. 2:14 NIV)

(And in my journal under this verse, I wrote, WHETHER IT SEEMS LIKE IT OR NOT!)

Honestly, girls, there are just plenty of moments when we think we know best, but our heavenly Father tosses out a holy curve and does things his way.

> *I am Jesus.* (Acts 9:5)

That's what he said to Saul and that's what he says to me when I get all upset about losing control and things not going my way. In other words, he has final say, and his way is *always* best—whether it appears so at the moment or not!

Because of that, it's always safe to run to him with your anger, frustration, confusion, and disbelief when he allows your plans to go topsy-turvy. In fact, there's no place safer. He knows how you feel anyway, and it's much healthier to lay it before him than to keep stewing inside.

God longs to fill you with his peace. He's not trying to upset you, but possibly trying to get your attention so that you can learn to trust him no matter how things appear.

The truth is, he is God and owes no one an explanation. Many times I do not understand why he allows some things to happen and why he doesn't seem to intervene in situations the way I think he should. I do know this: he allows circumstances in life to force us to give up control. And while we may not have control over those circumstances, we do have control over our response to them.

I believe there's a critical response time too. For me, if I immediately "give it back" to him, saying, *I don't understand, Lord, but I trust you,* I'm on the right track. But if I keep company—even for a short time—with disappointment and resentment, then it's more difficult for me to later birth that right attitude.

It all comes down to making the right and godly choice to trust God when everything in life seems to be going wrong. Perhaps he's trying to get your attention like he did with Saul. Just maybe he needs to "strike you blind" to get you to listen to him. To tell you the truth, I've had a couple of those blinding experiences when it seemed God was getting right in my face and blocking out my surroundings so I'd get the message.

I've decided to grow in the practice of paying attention to him and trusting him when things don't go according to my plans. Living a life of trusting God is much easier living and, in the long run, will save you from wasting your energy trying to figure out why it didn't go your way!

> *Lean on, trust in, and be confident in the Lord with all your heart and mind and do not rely on your own insight or understanding. In all your ways know, recognize, and acknowledge Him, and He will direct and make straight and plain your paths.*
> (Prov. 3:5–6 AMP)

- What areas in your life seem out of control?

- If you trusted God with that situation, would you feel more peaceful?

CHAPTER EIGHT

Controlling the People in Your Life

Search for the LORD and for his strength,
and keep on searching.

Psalm 105:4 NLT

When our son Lane was eight years old, our friend James was visiting in our home. "Dr. James" is a psychologist (we know how to pick friends!). One evening we were relaxing in the den and Lane scampered toward the back door saying, "I'll be back in at 8:15, Mom." For whatever reason, I thought his playtime outside should end at 8:00 instead. So the rest of the conversation went something like this:

Mom: "Be in at 8:00, honey."

Lane: "Aw Mom, just a *little* longer, please!"

Mom: "No, be in at 8:00."

Lane: "Just a little longer. How about 10 minutes after eight?"

Mom: "Come on in at 7:45."

Lane: "OK, I'll be in at 8:00."

As he scurried outside and I felt a smile of triumph tickle my lips, Dr. James asked, "May I make an observation?"

Always eager for free advice, I said, "Sure, bring it on."

"Have you ever considered yourself an either/or person?"

Curious, I remarked, "What do you mean?"

Sparing you the psychological jargon, what he basically said was that Lane was allowed his playtime, but it was either my way and on my terms or not at all. Well, I did agree that this was an accurate assessment of the situation. Later that night, I gave the whole either/or principle some thought.

How many other areas in my life was I strictly either/or? I realized there were many! I remembered that just the previous day I came home from teaching school and because I couldn't run the three miles I'd worked up to, I chose not to run at all. There were also times I remembered thinking, *Since I don't have time to clean the whole house today, I'm not going to clean anything.*

Probing the whole concept a little deeper, I realized that I'd been either/or with my husband, my coworkers, my students at school, and even on committees at church.

Was this trait of expecting things (and people) to conform to my way of thinking an area in my life that God wanted me to examine in the light of my love relationship with him? I believe so.

Back to the "be in at 8:00" issue. Parents are supposed to have things their way and on their terms, aren't they? Well—to a point. But there was no reason I couldn't have reasonably negotiated a few more minutes of playtime. In that particular situation, it would not have been illegal, immoral, or dangerous. And it would have shown my son that I was willing to take his desires into consideration.

To be truthful here, the parent thing just kicked in and said, *You have to let him know who's boss and that you have the final word in this situation.*

I'm happy to report that I did finally realize that it was OK to allow Lane, Brandon, and husband Larry to have the final say. I can hear them saying, "Now which two times were those?!" Really though, with practice I did get better at this. It's now easier for me to examine situations closely to determine if there's leeway in that final word—surprisingly enough, there often is!

So what is it about us that kicks in this need to control?

Some people may mistakenly believe their worth is dependent on other people and circumstances. You might have noticed that many insecure people are manipulators and controllers of others. There's this feeling of *If I'm in control of this person or this circumstance, it will make me look better. I will appear more successful and be held in higher esteem by others.*

As a child of God, your identity is in Jesus Christ, and when you feel secure in that identity, you don't need to control or manipulate other people to make you "look good."

It's also true that sometimes our controlling tendencies are born out of ignorance . . . like when my children were babies and I dressed them according to *my* body temperature. If I was cold, then they were dressed in warm clothing. This wasn't because I was insecure, but because I loved them and wanted them to be comfortable. My only measuring stick was my own comfort.

It's important to closely examine motives behind a controlling personality.

Sometimes our desire to control is within healthy limits. It's natural to want to be in control of your life and to have some control in the lives of others and the situations you encounter. But when there's an exaggerated emphasis on controlling people and situations, problems can certainly arise.

It's not healthy to be totally without control. Neither is it healthy or beneficial to be obsessed with control. God knows your heart and mind, and he holds the key to the balance between the two. Seeking his face continually in this area will help free you from unnecessary stress in your life, as well as keep you from dishing it out to others.

- In what areas of your life are you an either/or person?

- Do you need to seek God's guidance to balance the "control areas" in your life?

CHAPTER NINE

Positive Control

Test me, LORD, and try me; examine my heart
and mind. For Your faithful love is before my eyes,
and I live by Your truth.

Psalm 26:2–3

*Y*ou've been reading about the negative side of controlling tendencies. But there are times when being a take-charge-and-in-control kind of gal is right, and even godly!

Queen Esther shows us what a life committed to following God can accomplish. Because of her boldness and willingness to take charge in a precarious situation, an entire race was saved from destruction.

> *"Go and assemble all the Jews who can be found in Susa and fast for me. Don't eat or drink for three days, night and day. I and my female servants will also fast in the same way. After that, I will go to the king even if it is against the law. If I perish, I perish." So Mordecai went and did everything Esther had ordered him.*
>
> *On the third day, Esther dressed up in her royal clothing and stood in the inner courtyard of the palace*

facing it. The king was sitting on his royal throne in the royal courtroom, facing its entrance. As soon as the king saw Queen Esther standing in the courtyard, she won his approval. The king extended the golden scepter in his hand toward Esther, and she approached and touched the tip of the scepter. "What is it, Queen Esther?" the king asked her. "Whatever you want, even to half the kingdom, will be given to you."

"If it pleases the king," Esther replied, "may the king and Haman come today to the banquet I have prepared for them." The king commanded, "Hurry, and get Haman so we can do as Esther has requested." So the king and Haman went to the banquet Esther had prepared. While drinking the wine, the king asked Esther, "Whatever you ask will be given to you. Whatever you want, even to half the kingdom, will be done." Esther answered, "This is my petition and my request: If the king approves of me and if it pleases the king to grant my petition and perform my request, may the king and Haman come to the banquet I will prepare for them. Tomorrow I will do what the king has asked." (Esther 4:16—5:8)

The banquet for the king and Haman, his right-hand man, was the first step in exposing the evil plot to kill the Jews. Esther made a choice to take control of a situation only she could address. The queen had been advised of a plot to kill all the Jews. If there was any chance of sparing them, she was the one to make that happen. She did not enter this situation without fear and trembling. For any person, including the queen herself, to enter into the king's presence without being summoned meant certain death. Only if the king found favor with her at that moment, would her life be spared. Esther was willing to make this move on behalf of her people. *If I perish, I perish,* she said. With great courage, this beautiful Jewess queen boldly entered into the throne room and presence of her husband, a temperamental pagan king. Because of her faithful willingness to boldly take charge, her life and the lives of God's people were spared.

This was certainly a time when the right person needed to be in control! I'm sure you've realized that there are many times in your life when you do need to take charge and control the situation at hand.

To help you determine when to control and when to step back, it might be helpful to take a look at the characteristics of both the *obsessive* and *balanced controllers.*

Obsessive Controller

- fueled by fear

- seeks to control things to keep from being overwhelmed with anxiety

- often feels helpless

- appears not to trust others

Balanced Controller

- knows someone needs to take charge

- analyzes the situation

- takes time to think, pray, and act in obedience

- realizes God is ultimately in control

Living a *self-controlled* life is far different from living a life as a controlling person.

> *The fruit of the Spirit is love, joy, peace, patience,*
> *kindness, goodness, faith, gentleness, self-control.*
> (Gal. 5:22–23)

God begins to develop self-control in you as soon as the Holy Spirit takes up residence in your heart. You don't have to muster it up, but you *do* have to stop, think, and appropriate the power of Christ instead of reacting from your own natural tendencies.

Esther feared for her life and had every reason to do so. However, she had the presence of mind to stop, consider, wait, and plan her course of action. Based on Esther's response, and from observing others who have experienced victories in this area, I am offering some guidelines for you to consider.

If daily living for you is anything like it is for me, you'll have plenty of opportunities to put these guidelines into practice!

- **Pause.** Breathe deep and collect your thoughts. Instead of rushing into a situation, take time to think.

- **Pray Scripture.** Focusing on God's Word will always lead you in the right direction. Jeremiah 33:3 gives me great hope: "Call to Me and I will answer you and tell you great and wondrous things you do not know." God will lead you if you just ask him!

- **Seek counsel.** There are times when it helps to have a sounding board. This may be a trusted friend or a pastor. Pray with this person. If God wants you to seek another's opinion, he will lead you to the right person.

- **Stand still.** Sometimes the best way to take charge is to do nothing. Remember the truth of Exodus 14:14! "The LORD will fight for you; you need only to be still" (NIV).

- **Move in obedience.** After you've had time to consider and pray about the situation, move in the direction you feel God is leading. Be bold and confident, knowing you have sought his face through prayer, Scripture, and perhaps godly counsel. Trust him to lead you along the way. Be attentive to his direction, moving step by step as he leads.

There are also times when we must act immediately without opportunity to stop, think, and consult others. If you have spent time with Jesus daily, seeking his counsel and reading his Word, then I believe he will guide you in those split-second decisions. I can confidently say that he moves me in his will as I breathe a prayer and respond with him on my mind.

- What situations do you need to take charge of in your life?

- Which of the above guidelines will be most helpful to you?

CHAPTER TEN

Others Who Control

If possible, on your part, live at peace with everyone.

Romans 12:18

*A*s we move into the last chapter revolving around "control," I thought I'd share a comment from our friend Charlie Summers to our newlywed son: "Lane, let me give you a word of advice. You should ALWAYS have the final word: *Yes, ma'am!*"

Charlie's the man! Oh what a peaceful place the world would be if *everyone* agreed with *me!*

OK—but what if it's that *other* person who is insisting on being right? Take a look at what was going on between Cassie and Darla.

Cassie was sick and tired of feeling like this. Darla was her friend, in fact, probably her best friend. But lately she was getting on Cassie's last nerve! They had been through many things during the years and always seemed so compatible. Often they'd cried through their problems, only to end up laughing and sharing the deepest intimacies of their hearts. There was no one who knew and understood Cassie the way Darla did. There had always been much comfort, compassion, and gentleness in the way they responded to each other. Recently, however, Darla had taken on a new personality—a personality that really rubbed Cassie the wrong way. Darla was insisting on having her way in all their interactions. She seemed to have an agenda in every discussion and was always calling the shots about everything they did. She had moved from a warm, intimate friend to a person who was insisting on her way, never considering Cassie's opinion. She was turning into an absolute control freak!

Most of us have been around someone who seeks to control the people and circumstances around them. So what's a gentle, loving, and caring frazzled female to do? I believe if we take a look at what's behind the scene—you know, catch a glimpse of what's whirling around in that obsessed mind—we'd be a little more interested in wanting to get along with that *person in control!*

For many, close ties to a relationship or circumstances exacerbate controlling tendencies. When you care deeply about others, you want the best for them. And to the controlling person, that translates into telling people what choices they should make. If the controlling people are in the middle of circumstances that need attention, they may step up to the plate and take over. They feel their mission is to take charge, have the final word, and get things done right.

I'm not excusing this behavior. I'm just offering the probability that many people who seek to control have good intentions. When I realize that, it helps me be a little more tolerant (and Jesus-like) of their actions and compassionate of their needs.

You see, anxiety almost always fuels the need to control. The person who controls may not always admit or even realize that. But by seeking to control other people and situations, the controller is warding off fears of being helpless or having their control snatched away. As situations and people around us change, we can all become very vulnerable to taking on these tendencies.

I remember when my older son, Brandon, first left home. As I helped him move out of the house and watched him drive off, my mind was racing with *Who's going to take care of him? Will he eat right? Will he keep his apartment clean?* It was very difficult during our initial phone conversations not to harass him with all the things I wanted to make sure he was doing. As he moved out, my control over many things in his life moved with him.

This jurisdiction of control can change in a heartbeat. When control issues are changed, we become extremely vulnerable to fears and anxieties about being found helpless, useless, and well . . . *out of control!*

There are all sorts of controlling tendencies, and people seek to control for many reasons. I'm not a psychologist and couldn't possibly address the many facets of this disorder. I am, however, a frazzled female experiencing more and more of those wonderful victoriously frazzled moments through the power of Jesus Christ living in me! He is teaching me how to better love myself and how to better love those who surround me—even those who seem difficult at times to love.

Through my experience, I offer the following coping strategies. I'm realizing that through God's love and compassion, I can deal with all sorts of people. (I'm hoping they'll also follow these guidelines when dealing with *me!*)

- **Be Jesus-calm.** Controllers tend to generate a lot of tension. Keep your distance (physically and emotionally) so that you can stay focused when you speak to them. Your calm body language and speech will help them stay calm too.

- **Choose your words.** The normal tendency is to speak rapidly and loudly when you speak to those who are trying to get the upper hand. Deliberately slow your rate of speech and carefully choose your words. This will have a calming effect on you and the other person.

- **Practice patience.** Controllers need to be heard. Let them vent. Show them with your facial expressions that you care about them. Offer a few words to let them know you've heard what they've said. Remain calm until they've finished.

- **Be kind.** Pulling this piece of artillery from your arsenal will have unbelievable results. While the other person is building those defenses of anger and lashing out, offer nothing but kindness. There's nothing like kindness to jam up a full-fledged verbal attack.

- What controlling tendencies do you have, born out of anxiety?

- Does understanding this help you be kinder *to yourself* and feel more compassion toward others?

PART THREE

Responding God's Way

But thanks be to God, who gives us the victory
through our Lord Jesus Christ!

I Corinthians 15:57

*T*he last days of school always ushered in lots of emotions
for me as a middle school teacher. I was thrilled with the
rest that would soon be mine—for a short while, anyway.
Always, lots of tension and "guarded behavior" on my part,
wanting to keep that firm upper hand right until the final
hour.

So it was a real test for me on the first day of that last
week of school during my last year of teaching at Kings
Mountain Middle School. The test presented itself in the
form of paper wads thrown at me, in unison, and strategically planned by my last period class of sixth graders.
I loved those kids, even though it was kind of a put-your-
teacher-on-the-ceiling kind of relationship we shared.
We really had come a long way that year and had grown

together through writing tests, field days, along with day-to-day peer battles and challenges to adult authority.

That particular afternoon we walked back after lunch and into our classroom on the second floor. I noticed a peculiar sort of quietness settling over my usually hyper students, and there was a glint of mischief that I noticed in some eyes that early afternoon as I made my way up front to begin teaching that period of English students.

In one synchronized effort with planned determination, those carefully crafted wads of notebook paper blasted from every direction the second I opened my mouth to speak. It was a hurling fury of thirty well-aimed paper missiles splattering against my face in hearty unison.

Right there—a split second of response time that I held in my hands—was a teeny, little, fiery moment of a reaction opportunity. And it was one that strongly impacted the fate of those students for the remaining school days that year.

As I often did when teaching writing skills, I'm tempted just to "leave you here" and let you create your own version of the rest of this story. I know you could come up with all sorts of reasonable consequences for those *less than well-behaved* students who showed no fear for their teacher!

Even in writing about it now, I still can hardly believe my response. By nature I'm reactionary. That's why I feel the need to consistently take on the mind and ways of Christ! I can tell you that it was God who led me straight along the path of victory that day, because the outcome of that event cinched the relationship I had with those kids.

And the way he led was not a common sense kind of leading. I often notice that about my Lord. Read what Oswald Chambers said about common sense:

> *Common sense and faith are as different from*
> *each other as the natural life is from the spiritual, and*
> *as impulsiveness is from inspiration. Nothing that*

Jesus Christ ever said is common sense, but is revela-
tion sense, and is complete, whereas common sense
falls short.[3]

Common sense, at that moment, would have led me to pour forth the Wrath of Wood to these undisciplined students who had disrespected their teacher and acted impulsively and carelessly. They certainly deserved reprimand and the consequences (according to my behavioral management system) that went along with such rash behavior!

But what they got was a good dose of Jesus! Oh, they didn't know it, but I sure did! For moments I stood dumbstruck. They stared as they held their breath, waiting for what was to come. They'd betted on my reaction and were willing to take whatever the consequence (hoping I'd be merciful), in a trade-off for the shock factor.

As I broke out in laughter, their stiff bodies relaxed and they high-fived their classmates. What had been a potentially high-voltage moment of screaming rebuke on my part, turned into one that was lighthearted and gentle. And I can tell you, I sure needed some "playful" moments during those tension-packed last days of school.

Other times during that school year, that response on my part would not have been appropriate. Obviously, students should not normally get by with outbreaks of disrespect like that. But because of consulting my Lord during that "second of a response time," my students and I were spared the negatives of what could have been.

For me, choosing to respond instead of react was the best choice. We finished that class and made it through the rest of the classes that week. A new and deeper bond had been formed with Mrs. Wood and the sixth grade Wonderkids!

CHAPTER ELEVEN

Reacting Versus Responding

Set a guard over my mouth, O LORD; keep watch
over the door of my lips.

Psalm 141:3 NIV

Jan was leaving the grocery store, juggling three bags of groceries and a sack of guilt. All she could think was *I wish I had handled that differently!* She felt absolutely horrible! In fact, she felt pretty bad before she ever made it into the grocery store that afternoon. She hadn't slept well for days, so her nerves were already on edge when she rounded the corner and was hit head-on by the cart of an oncoming speed demon. Jan, who was usually calm and easygoing, screamed, "What is your problem!" Immediately her spirit crouched in shame as the older gentleman replied, "Forgive me, ma'am. My wife just got out of the hospital. She's in the car and I was afraid to leave her alone, but I had to pick up a few things for supper tonight. I shouldn't have been in such a hurry."

Ouch!

It's our tendency to have reactionary natures; then throw in all those stresses that pile up day to day, and it's pretty easy to understand why those explosive words roll out so easily.

In fact, there are often contributing factors that lead to volatile reactions. The same stress overload that weakens your immune system, making you more prone to sickness, also weakens your resolve to respond to situations in a Christlike manner.

So where are you on your personal stress Richter scale?

1	2	3	4	5	6
no reaction				over the top	

Could some of the following factors contribute to making you reactionary?

- not getting enough sleep

- hungry because of dieting

- worried about something

- stressed over too much to do

- grumpy because "nobody helps"

- feeling out of shape

- nerves on edge from dealing with so many things

- family is uncooperative

- house is dirty

- and . . . *ad infinitum*

Life certainly has a way of wearing you down, doesn't it? It's often difficult to keep your cool when everyone and everything seem to be going against the flow. When you don't feel well and nobody seems to be listening to you and life in general feels pretty rotten, it's just difficult to respond with the gentleness of Jesus.

Now's the time to kick in the plan. "Which plan is that?" you say. Well, it's the JESUS PLAN. Pure and simple, you learn to respond like Jesus even when you *don't feel like it.* How do you do this? You determine to. You think about situations ahead of time that could cause you to lose control, and you pray about those people and events. You make yourself aware of where you are on your personal stress scale and, if you can, you adjust your schedule. For instance, if you're weighing heavy on the stress side, you may want to avoid some situations or people— if possible—until you feel calmer. And if avoiding them isn't an option, you talk to the Lord about it. If you ask him, he *will* help you remain calm and respond with his gentleness. I often ask him to protect people from ME!

When I think of the gentleness of Jesus, I think of power under control.

I like that concept. It takes great strength to contain your wrath instead of lashing out. It's a Jesus thing to do, and it is his power, not yours, that enables you to respond this way.

You can read about this power under control in the eighth chapter of Luke, where Jesus rebuked the fury of a fierce windstorm, making it calm and gentle.

> *One day He and His disciples got into a boat, and He told them, "Let's cross over to the other side of the lake." So they set out, and as they were sailing He fell asleep. Then a fierce windstorm came down on the lake; they were being swamped and were in danger. They came and woke Him saying, "Master, Master,*

*we're going to die!" Then He got up and rebuked the
wind and the raging waves. So they ceased, and there
was a calm.* (Luke 8:22–24)

You see, when he rebuked that fierce windstorm, he
exhibited great power. But it was controlled power, not
power running rampant. His words were well chosen,
clearly spoken, and under control. What happened next?
The storm subsided and all was calm.

Oh how I long to respond like Jesus! Because of Jesus
living in me, I can be assertive instead of aggressively lashing out. I really can respond on the spot with power under
control. I can do this by allowing Jesus to do it for me!

Remember this. God wants you to respond with his
gentleness even more than you want to respond that way.
And he will help you do so, if you pause long enough to
think about him and consider his calmness before you
speak *or scream!*

- Have you ever *reacted* and felt horrible about it?

- Are you beginning to understand that spending
  time with Jesus on a regular basis will help you
  remain calm during unnerving circumstances?

- Are you willing to make time with him a priority
  in your life?

CHAPTER TWELVE

The Tongue of the Wise

A gentle answer turns away wrath,
but a harsh word stirs up anger.

Proverbs 15:1 NIV

*A*crowd gathered for a Christian music festival. With the music growing louder and the temperature growing hotter, one person in the crowd began dancing wildly and annoying those around him. Adam moved in and tapped the young man on the shoulder, asking him to calm down. Without warning, the guy spun around and sucker punched him, bloodying his nose. Adam steadied himself, regained his composure, looked his attacker squarely in the face, and said, "Hey man, this is a Christian concert, and you're not acting very Christlike. It's time for you to leave." Within moments the security personnel escorted him away. Adam is only twenty-one but has the spiritual maturity of one who has walked with the Lord for many years. Because of a godly response during an emotionally explosive moment, he was a tremendous witness for Jesus.

I want to be like Adam when I grow up! I am so impressed with the power of Jesus in his life. That kind of power doesn't just happen. It's not humanly possible to respond with the love of Jesus unless he lives in your heart and you've spent time with him learning his ways. The more you grow the lifestyle of being with Jesus on a daily basis, the more like him you'll become. Your personality will gradually take on his. His gentleness, compassion, and quiet strength will flow through you, and you will consistently become more like him. And when life throws you a sucker punch, you'll respond in his way, not yours! It's you *backing up* as he *takes over.*

A calm spirit makes all the difference in a volatile situation, doesn't it? When emotions are unstable and circumstances are unpredictable, it's easy to move into the defensive mode. For me that means short words and jerky reactions. In my natural state, I'm prone to a quick temper. It's taken years of prayer and dependence upon the Lord for me to learn to breathe in his presence before I jump into fight mode. Each time I take a deep breath and draw on the strength of the Lord instead of lashing out, I thank him for the victory! It's important to celebrate the victories each time they happen. It's an important reminder that you are making progress.

Keep in mind, this kind of growth does not happen overnight. That's OK. It will happen if you consistently go to that "quiet place" with him. Then, through a progression—a step-by-step process—you will notice that you are responding differently and feeling calmer than you used to. Jesus has a way of making the little things, *little*!

This verse from Proverbs helps me keep my focus.

> *A hot-tempered [woman] stirs up dissension, but a patient [woman] calms a quarrel.* (Prov. 15:18 NIV)

Now there's a good life-verse! Just looking back on my own life, I'm thinking, *Oooh—all the bad times that could have been avoided . . . if I'd only lived by that verse!*

Are you thinking the same thing? OK. No time for pining over those lost years. Get on with it! Start *now*, taking on the gentleness of Jesus. Now's the time for a new start—a fresh start with the Lover of your soul who will not only bring more joy and peace into your life, but will live his life through you so that you can minister to others with his peace and compassion.

When I'm learning a new skill—especially the *responding-like-Jesus* skill—it helps me to surround myself with reminders. Months ago during my quiet time with the Lord, he revealed a change I needed to make in my personality. It had to do with a negative thought pattern. Since it was a skill I had not yet mastered, I needed a frequent reminder to change my way of thinking. As this reminder, I chose a little black band to wear as a ring. All during the day when I noticed that little band, I remembered to apply my new thought pattern.

The same principle can be used for learning how to respond like Christ. If we don't think before we respond, and if we don't train ourselves to be like Christ, then we won't be like him and we won't respond like him. It doesn't come naturally, this being like Jesus. It takes training, discipline, and perseverance. We must place reminders in our paths to help us remember our goal.

When our children were young, I made a banner of Proverbs 15:1: "A gentle answer turns away wrath, but a harsh word stirs up anger" hung on our kitchen wall for years as a prominent reminder to respond to each other with love and gentleness instead of angry words. It wasn't decorative and it wasn't an impressive piece of artwork, but it was a big, beautiful truth that we tucked deeper into our hearts and minds each time we noticed it. As neighborhood children came in and out of our home, it was also a reflection of the love of Jesus for them too.

I'm so thankful that God's Word is filled with many reminders to help us learn about his character. He has also given us friends to remind us to stay on track. I encourage you to choose a friend as your accountability partner in this area. Share your vulnerabilities with her. Together you can laugh, maybe cry a little, and really encourage each other as you grow in the Lord!

- Are you a *hot-tempered woman* who stirs up anger or a *patient one* who calms a quarrel?

- Choose a verse for meditation. Notice how it helps you respond like Jesus.

- Find a "reminder," maybe like my little black ring, to help you respond like Jesus.

CHAPTER THIRTEEN

When Life Drives You Crazy

Therefore, we are ambassadors for Christ.

2 Corinthians 5:20

It was difficult for me to share the following story until I realized it really had nothing to do with me, but was all about Jesus!

A couple of years ago our son, Lane, was in a tragic automobile accident. Without the intervention of Jesus Christ, the outcome would have been devastating. Our mighty God miraculously healed all of Lane's body—a brain that had shifted and was hemorrhaging, a pelvis broken in four places, and lungs that had suffered trauma. We continue to praise God and adore him for what he did!

There was another miracle that occurred during those first hours, and it happened inside of me. Before the wreck I had just returned home from a 5:30 a.m. workout at our YMCA. Right after I walked in the door, we received the telephone call about Lane's wreck. Now I can look pretty rough in the morning, especially if I've been exercising.

After learning of my son's accident, this ol' body was not a pretty sight. During the next twenty-four hours my physical appearance really deteriorated, but the glory of the Lord exploded! Time and time again as we walked the halls next to the ICU unit in Charlotte, North Carolina, strangers walked up to me and remarked, "You are so beautiful." I remember running to find a mirror to take a look at what they could possibly be seeing!

Then it hit me. At those moments they were seeing the manifestation of Jesus!

Honestly, when I realized what was happening, I was overcome with emotion: My Lord, shining his glory during the middle of such tragic circumstances, left me loving him more than ever before.

When Jesus Christ "appears" in us and through other people, we should be humbled and awed, thankful—but never surprised! We know that he is with us and a part of each event we live through, so it should never surprise us when he manifests himself through us.

> *We are therefore Christ's ambassadors, as though*
> *God were making his appeal through us.*
> (2 Cor. 5:20 NIV)

That's precisely who we are supposed to be: Jesus in the flesh to a world who does not know him. And to those who do, we can be an encouragement of his love and his constant presence.

Sometimes when I'm around others, I can tell that Jesus lives inside of them by their facial expressions. Other times, I'll notice a godly response to a difficult circumstance. Sometimes it's silence that speaks, while at other times well-chosen words exhibit the presence of the Lord.

Anyone who has the Spirit of God living in him or her is free to exhibit the love of God. In other words, God's

Spirit frees us from worldly reactions and moves right into reflecting his glory.

> *Now the Lord is the Spirit; and where the Spirit of the Lord is, there is freedom. We all, with unveiled faces, are reflecting the glory of the Lord and are being transformed into the same image from glory to glory; this is from the Lord who is the Spirit.*
> (2 Cor. 3:17–18)

I always want the Lord to shine his glory through me. Truth is, it sure is easier when things in life are going smoothly. Reflecting the love of Jesus is no problem when life is going right and I'm feeling good. The real test comes when life is driving me crazy and that sinful nature kicks in. You know—that nature that's filled with worry, anger, fear, and STRESS! That's when the world is really watching, especially unbelievers. They're looking to see if our walk matches our talk. They're searching and hoping that Jesus does make a difference, because they're not too sure about the whole Christianity thing. During those times God makes his appeal through us.

The wonderful thing about the whole Jesus-showing-through-me issue is this: The only thing I have to do is love him more. The deeper my love relationship with him, the more I sink into his ways, not mine. Being like Jesus will gradually become more normal than not, the more intimate you become with him.

And you see—IT'S ALL ABOUT HIM, not about you.

Because of Christ living in you, you are a new creation. I like the word *new.* It makes me think of things fresh and untarnished. That's exactly who you are in Jesus. If Jesus lives inside of you, then you are in a position to reflect his glory.

> *Therefore, if anyone is in Christ, he is a new*
> *creation; the old has gone, the new has come!*
> (2 Cor. 5:17 NIV)

You can position yourself to reflect the glory of Jesus to the world around you by allowing the Lord to transform you into his likeness. The Lord does the transforming. That's his plan for you through Christ. He gives you the choice, however, to cooperate with his plan.

- What characteristics of Jesus do you want to show the world around you?

- Spending time loving him and talking with him will help you take on his ways. Are you experiencing this intimacy with Jesus?

CHAPTER FOURTEEN

When Others Are Unkind

"You have heard that it was said, Love your neighbor
and hate your enemy. But I tell you, love your enemies
and pray for those who persecute you."

Matthew 5:43–44

*J*anice stopped by the store to pick up a few things after
work. It had been a hectic day, and she felt tired and
grumpy from dealing with stressful situations. Walking into
the store, she passed Susan, who chaired the social committee at church. When Susan noticed her, instead of greeting
her with a smile and a "hello, friend," she quipped, "Have
you turned in your idea for the table decorations? They
were due last week, you know." Janice, already irritable
because of her hard day at work, paused. Instead of snap-
ping back, she caught her breath and slowly said, "Thanks
for the reminder. I'll do that when I get home."

Well! I would say that Janice was being like Jesus.
There are many verses in the Bible devoted to treatment of
others. Read these words of Jesus.

*Do not judge, so that you won't be judged. For
with the judgment you use, you will be judged, and*

with the measure you use, it will be measured to you.
Why do you look at the speck in your brother's eye but
don't notice the log in your own eye? Or how can you
say to your brother, "Let me take the speck out of your
eye," and look, there's a log in your eye? Hypocrite!
First take the log out of your eye, and then you will
see clearly to take the speck out of your brother's eye.
(Matt. 7:1–5)

It's easy to snap at people, and to feel justified in it when they treat you badly. It's especially easy to *let 'em have it* when you don't think you deserve their treatment. Some of those times when people have released their fury on me, I've been like Janice and caught myself before I blew up. There have been other times, however, when I quickly retaliated.

I'm always more pleased, though, when God gets the glory through a calm and gentle response, aren't you? Even though it may be more difficult at that moment, it's always gratifying to know that you responded like Jesus would have.

I believe that in the context of that Matthew 5 verse, when Jesus said to *love your enemy,* he was also talking about your friends who act unkindly and abruptly. You know, stress can make you do that. I've been the victim of somebody's stressed-out nature. I've also been on the giving end of that tongue lashing.

Whomever the enemy—one with ongoing hostility or a friend who reacts to the heat of the moment—Jesus said show love!

Proverbs 25 gives us radical instructions for dealing with our enemies:

If your enemy is hungry, give him food to eat,
and if he is thirsty, give him water to drink; for you

*will heap coals on his head, and the L*ORD *will reward you.* (vv. 21–22)

The idea of heaping coals on my enemy's head has always intrigued me. It's returning evil with good! If your enemy is hungry and thirsty, you can do for him what he doesn't deserve—give him food and water. The way to turn an enemy into a friend is to be friendly to him. That act of kindness to someone who doesn't deserve it is being . . . *so Jesus!*

(It helps me to remember the many kindnesses I have experienced from God when I didn't deserve them!)

Proverbs 25:22 tells us that if we heap those coals, the Lord will reward us. I can't think of a better reason to bite my tongue and lay my spirit down before another. I long to be rewarded by Jesus. And the greatest reward I receive is the realization that I have pleased him in my attitude and behavior.

If you can just get by that split second of injury—the moment of your attack—then you have the blessed opportunity of honoring Christ and then receiving his reward. That reward may be immediate, like sensing his victory of the moment. You also have continuing opportunities to lay up rewards in heaven by the way you respond to others.

Oh, the presence of mind to behave like Jesus!

Treat others as you want them to treat you. (Matt. 7:12 CEV)

Oh Lord, teach me to be like Jesus. Help me want to treat others the way you would treat them. Even if I don't deserve what they say to me and what they do to me, help me to show them your love!

- Is there someone in your life who needs to see Jesus in you?

- In what ways can you "heap some coals" today?

CHAPTER FIFTEEN

Reactions Worth Having

> The good man brings good things out of the good
> stored up in his heart. . . . For out of the overflow
> of his heart his mouth speaks.
>
> Luke 6:45 NIV

*D*eborah was a prophetess and judge for the nation of
Israel. She also went to war with them, bringing Israel
to victory and leading them in praise to God for the deliverance of his people.

> *Deborah, a woman who was a prophet and the*
> *wife of Lappidoth, was judging Israel at that time. It*
> *was her custom to sit under the palm tree of Deborah*
> *between Ramah and Bethel in the hill country of*
> *Ephraim, and the Israelites went up to her for*
> *judgment.*
>
> *She summoned Barak son of Abinoam from*
> *Kedesh in Napthtali and said to him, "Hasn't the*
> *LORD, the God of Israel, commanded you: 'Go,*
> *deploy the troops on Mount Tabor, and take with you*
> *10,000 men from the Naphtalites and Zebulunites?*
> *Then I will lure Sisera commander of Jabin's forces,*

> *his chariots, and his army at the Wadi Kishon to fight*
> *against you, and I will hand him over to you.'"*
>
> *Barak said to her, "If you will go with me, I will*
> *go. But if you will not go with me, I will not go."*
> *"I will go with you," she said, "but you will receive*
> *no honor on the road you are about to take, because*
> *the* LORD *will sell Sisera into a woman's hand." So*
> *Deborah got up and went with Barak to Kedesh.*
> (Judges 4:4–9)

What a woman! Deborah was quite impressive as she spoke with confidence and moved in the strength of the Lord. She spoke God's command to go into battle to the commander of the army, Barak. He reacted with fear and cowardice. But Deborah moved forward, standing shoulder to shoulder with Barak on the battlefield. When the commander of the army wavered, Deborah stood strong in her faith, trusting God to do what he said he would do, even though the odds seemed stacked against Israel. When victory was certain, Deborah reacted with gratitude and an overflowing heart full of praise. Her musical thanksgiving lifted the spirits of the Israelites and ushered them into praise to God for the greatness of his power.

In the previous chapters we've explored negative reactions that cause harm and inflict hurt. There are times, however, when reactions can have a positive effect.

Consider the following experience: One afternoon while walking through her neighborhood, Jean passed an acquaintance who lived several blocks away. She noticed the woman was teary-eyed and moving slowly. Immediately Jean gave her a hug and asked if she could help. She could have walked on, speaking briefly while ignoring her emotional state, or turned and walked the other way. Jean's reaction, however, was to offer concern and show compassion. As a result, she was able to show encouragement and make positive difference in her neighbor's life.

Reacting when God wants you to react is just as important as not reacting when he doesn't.

Personally speaking, it's easier to react in a godly way when I've had consistent time being with Jesus. Spending time with him helps me more accurately assess a situation, it seems. I just trust my "instincts" more when I've had time with him, studying the Bible and sensing the direction of his spirit.

I pray that I will be so steeped in Jesus that when those opportunities come to share his love, I'll move right in. I do believe it's very important to breathe a quick prayer before the approach! When an "opportunity of the moment" happens and there's not much time to pray, I do believe that the Holy Spirit will impress upon us what to do, if we quickly ask him. Only he knows the person, the situation, and how he wants us to react.

As you pray about the day ahead, there will be many situations that will not be specifically addressed in prayer. But he will help you as your day unfolds to respond like he would. By spending time with the Lord on a daily basis, you will begin to take on his characteristics. You will begin to think like him, behave like him, and react like him. It makes sense that if you saturate yourself in the Scriptures and the presence of God, you will be more likely to react like he would in any given situation.

I believe that's why Deborah was able to assertively bring Israel to victory in battle. She had been with God, seeking his direction, and then confidently stepped out in boldness to do what he said to do.

I know that spending time with the Lord each day builds my confidence and causes me to courageously do the things he directs me to do. When those daily stressors come my way, I'm aware when the grace of Jesus takes over. It's like a touch to my spirit before I speak or move. It's so *not* like me to be calm and serene in the middle of haphazardness. But the more time I spend with him, growing my love for him, the more I become aware of his presence directing my ways.

The best way to train yourself to respond and react like Jesus is to spend time with him consistently. Spending time in prayer and in the Scriptures equips you in ways no earthly method can. Talk to your heavenly Father about it. Ask the Holy Spirit to speak your words, move through your body, and shine on your face. Those are reactions worth having, and you'll attract the world around you to Jesus!

- Are your *on-the-spot* reactions typically positive or negative?

- How does being with Jesus affect the way you react to stressful situations?

PART FOUR

Experiencing God's Practical Power

He demonstrated this power in the Messiah by
raising Him from the dead and seating him at
His right hand in the heavens.

Ephesians 1:20

I love to speak about the practical power experienced in
a love relationship with Jesus Christ. For many years,
I did not understand the power available to me as a child
of God. I was like many Christians: I loved him and had
a good relationship with him, but I didn't really understand
the far-reaching practical applications for me personally in
my love relationship with Jesus.

I believe many Christians in describing God's love
would leave out the word *practical*. When I was first
enlightened regarding the practicality of God's love, I was

so excited, I could hardly stand it. This revelation came in the midst of a seminar for a Christian women's luncheon. I was speaking about how a relationship with Jesus could empower believers to be victorious in daily stressful activities. Here is the Scripture I read aloud to the women that day:

> *I keep asking that the God of our Lord Jesus Christ, the glorious Father, may give you the Spirit of wisdom and revelation, so that you may know him better. I pray also that the eyes of your heart may be enlightened in order that you may know the hope to which he has called you, the riches of his glorious inheritance in the saints, and his incomparably great power for us who believe. That power is like the working of his mighty strength, which he exerted in Christ when he raised him from the dead and seated him at his right hand in the heavenly realms.*
> (Eph. 1:17–20 NIV)

As I read that last sentence, *"That power is like the working of his mighty strength, which he exerted in Christ when he raised him from the dead and seated him at his right hand in the heavenly realms,"* my heart nearly jumped into my throat—THAT POWER IS AVAILABLE FOR ME WHEN I CLEAN MY BATHROOMS!

There is absolutely nothing in all of life that that power doesn't cover.

At that moment I took a gigantic spiritual step in my love relationship with Jesus, and ever since that sweet second of revelation, my heart still overflows with love and joy and *hope,* knowing that Jesus cares about all the diddly-squat things in my life!

Diddly-squat—now there's a spiritual concept! Just think of it, girls—not only is Jesus interested in those big events of life, he's just as interested in the mundane and "unextraordinary" minutes—day in and day out. I believe the devil himself is busy at work deceiving believers with lies like, "You don't need God for this; be ashamed. After all, he does expect you to do SOME things on your own."

I can't tell you how many women who come to Frazzled Female conferences think that God expects *them* to take care of the "little" things, leaving only the big ones to him! That lie is as far from the truth as it gets. First Corinthians 10:26 reminds us that "the earth is the Lord's, and everything in it." *Everything* includes little things.

Why would God's power not cover the little things when the accumulation of those little things often gives us the biggest stresses in life! When you grasp the following truths, your thinking about "God's interest in you" will be totally transformed, and everyday living will take on a new and spiritual meaning.

1. As a believer, God's power—the same power that he used when he raised Jesus from the dead—is available to you, and by using it you can live victoriously *every* day.

2. When you begin to appropriate his power, the mundane chores that fill up your days will take on new meaning. You will more easily understand and follow the directive given by Paul—and it will be a joy to do so!

> *And whatever you do, in word or in deed, do everything in the name of the Lord Jesus, giving thanks to God the Father through Him.* (Col. 3:17)

Now . . . on to the diddly-squat!

- In which areas of your life do you need to experience the practical power of God?

- In the accumulation of common daily hassles, what are some things that generally get the best of you?

Right now, ask him to make his power real in your life. Give thanks to him as you do *everything in the name of the Lord Jesus.*

CHAPTER SIXTEEN

God Loves to Surprise Us!

Take delight in the LORD, and He will give
you your heart's desires.

Psalm 37:4

*H*ave you ever had the experience of God speaking to you in an unlikely fashion? A couple of years ago the Lord touched my heart with a designer gift just for me and in a way that was very special.

When my husband wants to get my attention, he uses a certain whistle. And when he whistles, it seems I always hear him. It may be in a crowded room, or when he is standing above me on another level of the shopping mall, or it used to be above the endless chatter of our two boys when they were little. Even though he doesn't whistle loudly, it always gets my attention.

One day when I was walking through our neighborhood very burdened about some deep things going on in my life, I heard "the whistle." I know it seems weird, but I knew immediately that whistle was from my heavenly Father, and I sensed him saying, "I'm here. It will be OK."

One of my favorite Bible stories since I was a child is the one about the little boy Samuel. The Lord kept calling his name, but Samuel didn't recognize that it was him. I just bet God's heart was so delighted when Samuel finally recognized who was calling out to him. I do believe the Lord longs to delight us with his surprises!

> *The boy Samuel served the LORD in Eli's presence. In those days the word of the LORD was rare and prophetic visions were not widespread.*
>
> *One day Eli, whose eyesight was failing, was lying in his room. Before the lamp of God had gone out, Samuel was lying down in the tabernacle of the LORD where the ark of God was located.*
>
> *Then the LORD called Samuel, and he answered, "Here I am." He ran to Eli and said, "Here I am; you called me."*
>
> *"I didn't call," Eli replied. "Go and lie down." So he went and lay down.*
>
> *Once again the LORD called, "Samuel!"*
>
> *Samuel got up, went to Eli, and said, "Here I am; you called me."*
>
> *"I didn't call, my son." he replied. "Go and lie down."*
>
> *Now Samuel had not yet experienced the LORD, because the word of the LORD had not yet been revealed to him. Once again, for the third time, the LORD called Samuel. He got up, went to Eli, and said, "Here I am; you called me."*
>
> *Then Eli understood that the LORD was calling the boy. He told Samuel, "Go and lie down. If He calls you, say, 'Speak, LORD, for Your servant is listening.'" So Samuel went and lay down in his place.*
>
> *The LORD came, stood there, and called as before, "Samuel, Samuel!"*
>
> *Samuel responded, "Speak, for Your servant is listening." (1 Sam. 3:1–10)*

Not only was young Samuel caught off guard by God's voice, he didn't even recognize it was the voice of God speaking. First Samuel 3:7 says that "the word of the LORD had not yet been revealed to him." Verse 1 tells us "the word of the Lord was rare and precious in those days" (AMP).

Some time ago I went through a period when it seemed God was distant and I couldn't feel his presence or sense his nearness. *Where are you, Lord?* I thought. I just wasn't experiencing the closeness with him that I had once had, and I really needed to hear his voice.

Talking with others, I know my experience is not uncommon. There are many reasons why Christians may go through times of feeling distant from God. One of the most powerful lessons I have learned through these trying times is that I must never base my relationship with Jesus solely on my feelings. If I do, my feelings might tell me he has betrayed me and is no longer interested in me. That will never be true!

There are just times in life when we're like Samuel, *waiting for the word of the Lord to be revealed.* Or maybe he's speaking all around us and we are just not recognizing his voice.

It's important to always keep in mind that God loves you very much whether you *feel* his love at the moment or not. He loves you during the good times and bad times; he loves you when you rebel or when you are simply immature, spiritually speaking. It is not accurate to base God's love on how you feel. Sometimes those feelings will line up with his, but plenty of other times—what *you feel* has nothing to do with the way God feels about you!

If you are experiencing a time when God seems far away, I encourage you to keep pressing on. Keep seeking his face through studying and meditating on his Word, and keep that private and personal love relationship alive by worshipping him throughout your day. Ask God to reveal and remove any barriers to your relationship with him and to bring you back into close fellowship with him. Cry out with the words of the psalmist:

> *Restore to me the joy of your salvation.*
> (Ps. 51:12 NIV)

Be patient and diligent in your love life with Jesus, and your joy will return.

When he realized that it was God speaking to Samuel, the old priest Eli helped "position" Samuel to hear God's voice. In other words, he alerted Samuel to the fact that God was speaking to him and told him to simply respond to the voice saying, "Speak, LORD, for Your servant is listening" (1 Sam. 3:9).

Maybe you, dear friend, need a reminder today that God loves you and is speaking to you. Allow me to be your Eli. I'm telling you that God loves you and is pursuing a love relationship with you, one that is designed specifically for you and him! He wants you to hear his voice so that together you may share in the delights of his love. He's longing for you to welcome him into your daily life of places to go, things to do, and people to take care of. He wants to be your EVERYTHING!

- It is faulty theology to base God's love for you solely on your feelings. In which areas of your life are you doing that?

- What can you do today to "position" yourself to hear God's voice?

CHAPTER SEVENTEEN

The Ebenezer Stone

Be glad in the LORD and rejoice, you righteous ones;
shout for joy, all you upright in heart.

Psalm 32:11

*I*t's important to remember those times when God delivers us through trying circumstances. God intervenes throughout our lives in various ways. Sometimes I know he's speaking directly to me through something a friend says. Just this past week, I was feeling panicky about meeting a critical writing deadline. My friend Debbie had been praying over my speaking and writing schedule. She called one morning and offered a simple solution to help me work through some of my time issues. I was amazed. The answer was right there in front of me, but I hadn't figured it out. God revealed his direction through the voice of my dear friend.

Other times I've experienced his help when he provides a much needed parking space, when he opens a new grocery line just for me, and when that certain Scripture comes to my attention right at the time I'm needing it!

You've had these moments too, I know. I'm learning to celebrate them—big and small. They are *all* love gifts from Jesus and should be acknowledged as such. I'm so overwhelmed and grateful to my Lord that he just keeps pouring them on. I've discovered, too, that the more I notice them and thank him, the more often he sends them. Yes, how Jesus loves to delight our hearts.

The following passage from the Old Testament came alive for me years ago. You'll read about a "grown-up Samuel" still listening to God call his name. He had moved into a lifestyle of being with God and recognizing his voice. It was quite expected that he moved forth in obedience, following the Lord's directives in leading the nation of Israel.

> And Samuel said to the whole house of Israel, "If you are returning to the LORD with all your hearts, then rid yourselves of the foreign gods and the Ashtoreths and commit yourselves to the LORD and serve him only, and he will deliver you out of the hand of the Philistines." So the Israelites put away their Baals and Ashtoreths, and served the LORD only.
>
> Then Samuel said, "Assemble all Israel at Mizpah and I will intercede with the LORD for you." When they had assembled at Mizpah, they drew water and poured it out before the LORD. On that day they fasted and there they confessed, "We have sinned against the LORD." And Samuel was leader of Israel at Mizpah.
>
> When the Philistines heard that Israel had assembled at Mizpah, the rulers of the Philistines came up to attack them. And when the Israelites heard of it, they were afraid because of the Philistines. They said to Samuel, "Do not stop crying out to the LORD our God for us, that he may rescue us from the hand of the Philistines." Then Samuel took a suckling lamb and offered it up as a whole burnt offering to the LORD.

*He cried out to the LORD on Israel's behalf, and the
LORD answered him.*

*While Samuel was sacrificing the burnt offering,
the Philistines drew near to engage Israel in battle.
But that day the LORD thundered with loud thunder
against the Philistines and threw them into such a
panic that they were routed before the Israelites. The
men of Israel rushed out of Mizpah and pursued the
Philistines, slaughtering them along the way to a point
below Beth Car.*

*Then Samuel took a stone and set it up between
Mizpah and Shen. He named it Ebenezer, saying,
"Thus far has the LORD helped us."*
(1 Sam. 7:3–12 NIV)

This was truly an unlikely victory for the Israelites.
They had come together to fast and pray, not to fight. They
were unarmed and unprepared for war. Unarmed, earthly
speaking, that is. For they had come to God with hearts
full of repentance and determination to walk, once again,
in his ways. God heard their cries and honored the petition
of Samuel.

I continue to get so excited about new things the Lord
teaches me in his Word. One of the "new things" I learned
from this passage has greatly impacted my worship time
with him. I'm also becoming a more grateful recipient as
God lavishes his love. Just as he did with the Israelites,
there are times in my life when he rushes right into terrible
circumstances and explodes his victory!

Yep, God did something that only he could do. And
how did Israel respond? Samuel led them in erecting a
thankful memorial of this victory. It was to remind them
and to encourage them that God is faithful and does intervene in life's circumstances. The Ebenezer—"the stone of

help"—was set up in the same place where twenty years
earlier the Israelites were smitten by the Philistines.

While studying this passage from 1 Samuel, I was
impressed to spend some time thinking back through my
life about times when God seemed to rush to help me.
I began listing those in my journal. Each time I recorded
one event, another one came to mind. As my list grew, so
did my thankfulness! I experienced a fresh realization of
the sweetness of Jesus. He so wanted to be my helper, my
strengthener, my comforter.

I completed my "thankfulness journey" by collect-
ing beautiful little polished stones from the mines in the
North Carolina mountains and placing them in a small
bag. In my journal, I designated different colored stones
to stand for each event. My collection of Ebenezer stones
in my Ebenezer bag helps me remember to thank God for
his help in my past, knowing he will continue to help me
in my future!

My monuments of victory when God rushed to help
me include:

- Second Corinthians 4:18 being placed in my heart
  while I was with my mom in the hospice unit right
  before she died: "So we fix our eyes not on what
  is seen, but on what is unseen. For what is seen is
  temporary, but what is unseen is eternal" (NIV).

- Running across an index card with Hebrews
  10:35–36 written in my handwriting. I found it
  during a difficult day of writing. "So do not throw
  away your confidence; it will be richly rewarded.
  You need to persevere so that when you have
  done the will of God, you will receive what he has
  promised" (NIV).

- A small little car (instead of a stone) was found in my pocket one day. I was missing my little boy Brandon who is now grown up and moved away. It was a little car belonging to him, and I hadn't seen it for many years. Finding it made me smile and "get on with my day."

- A piece of the X-ray taken of our son Lane's brain after his accident reminds me how the Lord shifted his brain back to normal.

There are so many areas in my life where I can look back and praise God for his faithfulness. How honoring it must be to him when we remember all he has done for us. When I go back and review my Ebenezer moments, my heart fills with gratitude and I just worship him all over again.

- What is an event in your life—big or little—when God rushed in to help?

- When you think about those past times, what sorts of emotions fill your heart?

CHAPTER EIGHTEEN

Holy Spirit, I Need You!

"When the Spirit of truth comes, He will guide
you into all the truth."

John 16:13

*L*aurie dreaded the phone call she had to make. For weeks she had struggled with the decision to put her grandmother in a nursing home. In order to reserve the room, today was the last day to put in the request for the reservation. She had gathered facts about nursing home facilities, as well as spending much time assessing her grandmother's needs. She felt that she was pretty informed, but still had the unsettling feeling of not quite knowing if this was the right thing to do. In a flashback, she remembered reading in a daily devotional about the role of the Holy Spirit in giving guidance. She vaguely remembered where the passage was when Jesus said he would send his spirit to help us. After some searching, she located this verse in her Bible:

*I will ask the Father, and He will give you
another Comforter (Counselor, Helper, Intercessor,
Advocate, Strengthener, and Standby), that He may
remain with you forever.* (John 14:16 AMP)

I'm often like Laurie—needing some help in my life! Let's examine the Scriptures to find out what Jesus says about his spirit, who will help us in making those daily decisions.

> *If you love Me, you will keep My command-*
> *ments. And I will ask the Father, and He will give*
> *you another Counselor to be with you forever. He is*
> *the Spirit of truth. The world is unable to receive Him*
> *because it doesn't see Him or know Him. But you do*
> *know Him, because He remains with you and will be*
> *in you. I will not leave you as orphans; I am coming*
> *to you.* (John 14:15–18)

With all my heart I believe the words of Jesus apply to you and me today. If you have accepted Jesus into your heart as the Lord of your life, then you and the Holy Spirit have entered into a living relationship. He resides in you and is constantly with you. He is your personal counselor, your helper, your advocate, your strengthener, and your standby. You have the opportunity to turn to him, to seek his direction in every area of your life.

You're part of a beautifully power-packed love relationship with Jesus Christ! That power is available to change your life in personal areas, such as family relationships and emotional distresses. This power can also help you work through the countless things on your never-ending To-Do list. And with each victory, Jesus is glorified.

In regarding the filling of the Holy Spirit, Billy Graham puts it this way:

> The purpose of filling is that those who are
> filled may glorify Christ. The Holy Spirit came
> for this purpose. Jesus said, "He shall glorify Me;
> for He shall take of Mine, and shall disclose it to

you" (John 16:14). That is, the Holy Spirit does not draw attention to himself, but to Christ.[4]

When we acknowledge God's spirit in our lives and move forth from his promptings, God is glorified. It's a beautiful way to live—getting help to make it through difficulties and then glorifying Christ along the way.

Mr. Graham goes on to say that "a person who is filled with the Spirit may not even be conscious of it. Not one biblical character said, 'I am filled with the Spirit.' Others said it about them, but they did not claim it for themselves. Some of the most godly people I have known were not conscious that they were filled with the Spirit."[5]

When Jesus lives in you and you spend time with him on a daily basis, you can expect the Holy Spirit to direct you in each and every decision you make as you go through your day. You must remember to consult him, however.

James 4:2 says, "You do not have because you do not ask." So *asking for his help* is critical.

I remember taking my elderly grandmother to her favorite restaurant to eat. It was after a doctor's appointment, and we arrived right at lunchtime. When I approached the parking lot, it was full and I prayed aloud, "Lord, give us a parking space right up front." As I turned into the lot, a space right in front of the door became vacant. My grandmom and I laughed and talked about how the Holy Spirit opened that place just for us! We made three more trips to that restaurant during the next couple of months. Each time we pulled up to see a lot full of cars, and each time one pulled out right up front where we needed it. It was so fun celebrating the work of our helper, the Holy Spirit. So faith building too! To me, it was another awesome reminder of how God longs to be involved in our lives in practical ways. And parking spaces being provided—now that's practical!

You may not get a specific answer to your request, but many times you will. Other times you will sense his guidance as he impresses you in a certain way. Then you need to follow up in obedience. He may lead you to carry through with something or not to do something. He may impress you to change your attitude about a certain matter or apologize to a friend. He may simply want you to thank him for filling you with his peace and freeing you from worry. I can't list all the ways he might speak to you, but I can assure you that he will.

We are incapable of living the Christian life on our own. That's why at the moment of salvation, God sent his Holy Spirit to indwell us and *live for us,* the holy life of Christ.

> *And I no longer live, but Christ lives in me. The life I now live in the flesh, I live by faith in the Son of God, who loved me and gave Himself for me.*
> (Gal. 2:20)

We always have a choice, however, to submit to the control of the Holy Spirit. It's our choice to cooperate with him by allowing him to control us rather than give in to our fleshly desires.

You can know this about the power of the Holy Spirit:

- If Jesus is your personal Lord and Savior, the Holy Spirit lives in your heart.

- He wants to help you.

- You can ask him for help.

As you acknowledge his presence, thank him for being involved in your life. Then, know with confidence that your *Comforter, Counselor, Helper, Intercessor, Advocate,*

Strengthener, and Standby will remain with you forever. That's the promise of Jesus!

- In what area(s) of your life do you need help from the Holy Spirit?
- What would you like for him to do?

Maybe you'd like to pray this prayer:

Dear Jesus, Thank you so much for the gift of your Spirit living in me. Forgive me for not always acknowledging your Spirit's presence in my life. Right now I ask you to make me more aware of your Spirit and teach me to ask you for specific help as I go through my day.

CHAPTER NINETEEN

Speaking His Word

If you confess with your mouth, "Jesus is Lord," and believe in your heart that God raised him from the dead, you will be saved. For it is with your heart that you believe and are justified, and it is with your mouth that you confess and are saved.

Romans 10:9–10 NIV

I met Karen in a remote little town in Virginia during a Frazzled Female retreat. What I saw happen to her and the power—the practical power—that was manifested in her still grips my heart. We gathered around to sing praise songs after supper on the first night of out retreat. I noticed that Karen was not singing, so I offered to share my music with her. She responded dryly, "I don't sing." Something in her countenance led me to be very troubled in my heart about that comment. Later that evening Karen asked to talk with me. She shared about the troubling events going on in her life, as well as difficult issues she had struggled with as a child.

"I don't sing" kept coming to my mind.

Excited and hopeful, I said, "Karen let's try something. I believe that God wants you to sing."

She looked at me with disbelief, becoming visibly annoyed. She had just poured her heart out to me, and I was talking to her about singing! I knew, however, what the Holy Spirit had impressed upon my heart, so I insisted that we try singing together.

I sang, "God, you're so good . . ." and no Karen. She just looked at me as we held hands together, her eyes filling with tears. Finally, in the middle of sobs, she very quietly opened her mouth and began audibly praising God through song.

Karen and I sang for the next ten minutes. We both began to laugh and cry as we sang beautiful little choruses to the Lord. It seemed that I could see her being freed from bondage—emotional and spiritual bondage. She knew Jesus as her Savior but was not speaking his name aloud in praise.

The following day she shared, "You know, you were right about the singing aloud thing. I have been singing to God in my heart, but I needed to praise him aloud. This has made all the difference in the world. I feel like I've been set free!"

That incident was a powerful testimony to me—a testimony of God's desire to "hear" our praise. It's wonderful to have the praise of God living in our hearts, but I believe it's a double whammy aimed right at Satan when we shout God's praise, sing God's praise, and pray the Scriptures aloud. I've been determined since this experience with Karen to give audible praise to God for who he is and for what he's done!

Singing is a way to vocally show appreciation to our Lord. He gave us music, and that music is a beautiful way to communicate with him. Sometimes, just like Karen, people think, "I can't sing."

Ohhh, but you can! If you are blessed with vocal chords, you can sing. You just open your mouth and let it out! You are not singing for others, you are singing to Jesus! You are not performing, you are worshipping. And furthermore, the Holy Spirit takes those notes of praise and lifts them in beautiful holy harmony straight to the heavenly throne! It's his work, not yours, that transforms your offering into a beautiful gift of adoration. Your part is to let it pour forth out of your mouth.

Oh yes! When you sing you are being appreciative and obedient to your heavenly Father. You are following biblical instruction when you lift your voice in song!

> *Sing to the LORD, all the earth. Proclaim His salvation from day to day.* (1 Chron. 16:23)

I'm also growing in the practice of saying Scripture aloud throughout the day. Saying the verses and references out loud as I memorize helps me focus and more easily commit them to memory.

A friend of mine gave me a copy of *Praying the Bible* by Wesley and Stacey Campbell. The following paragraph made me chuckle:

> I am often in the habit of asking people a semi-trick question—do you know why God wants you to pray the Bible out loud? After I ask this question, people tend to look at one another questioningly. Pausing for dramatic effect, I reply: So you know when you've stopped! This usually takes a moment to sink in and then they all begin to snicker at one another. If you think about it for a moment, you will see the simple wisdom of this statement. It is hard to think about something other than what you're talking about. Praying out loud solves the problem of the wandering mind.[6]

Confessing means "saying the same thing as, or agreeing with." So when you "confess with your mouth" praise to God through singing or reciting Scripture, you are verbally saying the same thing as God and agreeing with him.

In agreement with God, I often confess, "I can do everything through him who gives me strength" (Phil. 4:13 NIV).

Confessing the Word of God in agreement with his Holy Spirit gives me much confidence for the task that lies ahead.

When I pray (confess) Scripture aloud, I sometimes reword it, making it personal to me. Here's how I pray the Philippians 4:13 verse: "Lord, I can do everything through YOU who gives me strength!"

Here's another example: "And whatever you do, in word or in deed, do everything in the name of the Lord Jesus, giving thanks to God the Father through Him" (Col. 3:17). When I personalize this verse, it becomes, "Whatever I do, in word or in deed, I do everything in the name of the Lord Jesus, giving thanks to God the Father through him."

As you move into the lifestyle of confessing Scripture aloud throughout the day, you'll find your focus shifting from your problems to your God. There is tremendous power available when we audibly acknowledge the goodness of our Lord—through song, through praise, and through Scripture.

- Does your mind usually wander during Bible reading?

- If so, how do you think reading aloud would help you stay focused?

CHAPTER TWENTY

Early Morning Quiet Time

Let me experience Your faithful love in the morning,
for I trust in You. Reveal to me the way I should go,
because I long for You.

Psalm 143:8

*L*eslie got up a half hour earlier than usual. She really wanted to draw close to Jesus and experience his presence in her life more than she ever had before. Now here she was at 5:30 a.m. with her Bible and her journal, ready to spend time with Jesus, and she thought, *Here I am, but what do I do?*

Leslie is one of many who attend Frazzled Female events. These women have listened to the teaching, they have committed to growing their love for the Lord, but they aren't quite sure what to do when they "arrive" at their appointment with Jesus!

Oh, what a wonderful problem to have! The Holy Spirit is so eager to lead you and guide you as you grow your "love time" with your heavenly Father. This first step of commitment is a beautiful one. It reminds me of working with ministry leaders in churches who have never had a women's event before. I sense an excitement and expectancy in their spirits as they try to organize and plan for the *perfect* event. It's also very common that these same women say to me, "We are so nervous because we've never done this before and we want to do it right." My heart just overflows with love and joy for them. It seems I feel a certain tender spot in the heart of our Lord for them because they are experiencing something fresh and new and not getting caught in the rut of "We've always done it this way!"

All that to say, YEA FOR YOU!

I hope you feel wonderfully excited that you are now entering into the most glorious love relationship of your life! To help you get an idea of what you're getting into, let me lay out some areas, as I see them, that give insight into the *"quiet place."*

- **Quiet.** I call it that because, in a huge sense, that's what it is. You pull away from all the clamor of the outside world, as well as resting from the distractions in your mind—you know, those inner voices.

    "Come with me by yourselves to a quiet place and get some rest." (Mark 6:31 NIV)

- **Early morning.** Jesus modeled this early morning prayer time while on Earth. Scriptures support seeking the Lord in the morning. Physically you are more rested and the day hasn't yet hit you. For me, it's honoring God when I give him the first part of my day, showing him that he is priority in my life!

> *Very early in the morning, while it was*
> *still dark, Jesus got up, left the house and*
> *went off to a solitary place, where he prayed.*
> (Mark 1:35 NIV)

• **Time of worship.** This includes singing to him,
reading Scripture, journaling your thoughts and
prayers, thanking him, interceding for others,
talking with him about your day ahead, sitting
still or kneeling while thinking of his attributes,
playing a musical instrument, dancing, and . . .
anything else offered to him in love.

> *I will sing to the LORD all my life; I will*
> *sing praise to my God while I live. May my*
> *meditation be pleasing to Him; I will rejoice*
> *in the LORD.* (Ps. 104:33–34)

• **Supplementary materials.** There are wonderful
Bible studies and devotional books and magazines
that are available to guide you through your *quiet-*
time experience. I encourage you, however, to take
periodic breaks from these "programs." Each of us
must be careful that we do not let someone else's
spiritual experience be a substitute for our own.
There are times I pull back from all devotional
aids and spend time in the Scripture, talking with
the Lord as I read.

> *Let the word of Christ dwell in you richly*
> *as you teach and admonish one another with*
> *all wisdom, and as you sing psalms, hymns*
> *and spiritual songs with gratitude in your*
> *hearts to God.* (Col. 3:16 NIV)

One woman in a recent session commented that she didn't want her quiet time with Jesus to become just another habit. I understand what she means, but the truth is—we need godly habits in our life!

Habits are behaviors that become routine because we do them over and over. Routine in the way of consistency in our spiritual life is very important! As we discipline ourselves to praise God, speak Scripture aloud, study the Bible, along with any other spiritual behaviors that we do consistently—we will create godly habits. You see, doing something one time does not produce long-lasting spiritual results. But doing it over and over until it becomes habit establishes a pattern that we learn to live by.

What you begin as a godly habit can lead you deeper into your love relationship with your Lord. When you faithfully and consistently meet him at that quiet place, worshipping him with a heart full of love, that godly discipline will turn into a love gift, one you can hardly wait to give him!

Let me offer some encouragement here. As you enter into this time of daily commitment, it may feel awkward. For me, it took a while to learn to be quiet and still. That's just not the kind of person I am. Just keep at it. It will get easier, the distractions will lessen, and you'll get more comfortable in "this place." Remember, the Holy Spirit will help you in growing this love relationship too. Just relax and enjoy each day of the journey.

You may find it helpful to have a guideline to follow. The following list helped me establish an early morning routine. As time passed, I added some other things as well. But for the most part I still begin my days like this:

- I pray Psalm 143:8: "Cause me to hear Your loving-kindness in the morning, for on You do

I lean and in You do I trust. Cause me to know the way wherein I should walk, for I lift up my inner self to You" (AMP).

- Next, I spend time thanking him. Often, I mentally go through the previous day, thanking him for how he was involved in each event, conversation, errand, and so forth. I thank him for saving me and for pursuing a love relationship with me.

- I offer him a repentant heart seeking forgiveness for specific sins and for missing the mark of holiness in certain thoughts and behaviors.

- I welcome the present-day ministry of the Holy Spirit—asking him to intervene in the specifics, whatever they are, in the day ahead.

There's no perfect plan or magical formula for spending time in this quiet place with the Lord. Just go. Be with him. Draw near to him and experience the blessings!

Draw near to God, and He will draw near to you. (James 4:8)

- In committing to a daily quiet time, what are possible obstacles for you?

- What gifts of worship could you offer the Lord?

- How will drawing near to God help grow your love for him?

PART FIVE

Yikes—I'm Getting Old!

So we're not giving up. How could we! Even though on the outside it often looks like things are falling apart on us, on the inside, where God is making new life, not a day goes by without his unfolding grace. These hard times are small potatoes compared to the coming good times, the lavish celebration prepared for us. There's far more here than meets the eye. The things we see now are here today, gone tomorrow. But the things we can't see now will last forever.

For instance, we know that when these bodies of ours are taken down like tents and folded away, they will be replaced by resurrection bodies in heaven—God-made, not handmade—and we'll never have to relocate our "tents" again. Sometimes we can hardly wait to move—and so we cry out in frustration. Compared to what's coming, living conditions around here seem like a stopover in an unfurnished shack, and we're tired of it! We've been given a glimpse of the real thing, our true home, our resurrection bodies! The Spirit of God whets our appetite by giving us a taste of what's ahead. He puts a little of heaven in our hearts so that we'll never settle for less.

That's why we live with such good cheer. You won't see us drooping our heads or dragging our feet! Cramped conditions here don't get us down. They only remind us of the spacious living conditions ahead. It's what we trust in but don't yet see that keeps us going. Do you suppose a few ruts in the road or rocks in the path are going to stop us? When the time comes, we'll be plenty ready to exchange exile for homecoming.

(2 Cor. 4:16–5:8 *The Message*)

CHAPTER TWENTY-ONE

We're All Getting Older

"I will be the same until your old age, and I will bear
you up when you turn gray. I have made you, and I will
carry you; I will bear and save you."

Isaiah 46:4

One summer day a couple of years ago, my (now) daughter-in-law Meghan and I were having some girl talk at our kitchen bar. We were laughing and talking about the way things used to be, when all of a sudden Meg blurted out, "Oh my gosh! I'm getting so old." I laughed at her outburst. Being up almost three decades in addition to her two, I had to agree. Life indeed was forging ahead and taking us with it.

I reflected on our conversation for the rest of the day. Meg's statement rang loudly, the sentiment of every woman past her teens—*I'm getting old!*

Truth is, we are all getting older. With each month, year, day, and minute we are inching along our earthly time line. The good thing about growing older is that we *are* growing older! Even considering the parts of the body that droop, drag, and stretch (not to mention the things that disappear, like well-toned skin and memory), there's much to be said about tucking experiences under our belts and knowing more than we used to.

Very likely, you have weathered some challenges that those younger than you haven't yet experienced. Depending upon your age, you know some things about loss, learning by doing, the challenges of singleness or married life or raising children or not being able to have children, and more. You probably know more than your younger sisters about making it through those rough times with the Lord's help. Then there are those lessons learned by sheer faith and placing your trust in him. Hopefully you have more wisdom, more stamina (spiritually, maybe not physically), and more insight into the deeper things of life.

> *[Our God] has made everything beautiful in its time. He also has planted eternity in men's hearts and minds (a divinely implanted sense of a purpose working through the ages which nothing under the sun but God alone can satisfy).* (Eccl. 3:11 AMP)

This is true about YOU! You are beautiful in his time! Whatever age you are, it's the right age for you right now. God has a purpose designed for you at this time of your life that is different from any other time of your life. Make sense? Right now is the perfect time for you, right now!

Much earlier in my life, God placed in my heart the passion to teach women. The motivation was there. The desire was there. The longing was in place. The only element missing was opportunity. Oh, I gain so much insight by looking back on those years and reading my "heartcries" in my journal. I was confused and bewildered about why the doors of ministry were not opening. I knew God was giving me a dream, but I was totally confused about why it wasn't happening.

Now I do know why those doors of ministry did not open at that time of my life. God's plan for me was to bump and bruise my way through some difficult tests and trials so I could be qualified for what I was about to teach. In other words, the timing was not yet right!

You see, your heavenly Father uses everything in your life to grow your experience, faith, and love for him! And there's no other way to develop those qualities except growing through them and growing older. No matter your age right now, you are in the process of growing within God's plan.

> *There is an occasion for everything, and a time for every activity under heaven.* (Eccl. 3:1)

The *now* in your life is a glorious place and an important place! I believe we spend too much time thinking about the final goal and what's next, instead of focusing on the present. I had those tendencies even as a child. I remember my dad saying to me during our family vacation: "Little girl, enjoy what we're doing right now, instead of worrying about what we're going to do next!"

Often I sense my heavenly Father saying to me:

> *Where you are right now, this very moment, is what's important to me. Don't worry about tomorrow and don't fret over yesterday. Don't focus on what's going to happen. Love me* now. *Trust me* r *Worship me* now, *and delight in me* now.

"Now o'clock" is the most important time have!

So what does this have to do with get seems to me our society overemphasizes th life, whatever that may be. For the child, i for the teenagers, it's young adulthood; fc

it's midlife; for the midlifers, it's retirement. We just always seem to be focusing on the *what next*.

Please don't misunderstand. I'm not suggesting we toss aside plans and preparations for what's to come. I'm just saying we should enjoy living in the present. Spiritually speaking, it has become so freeing for me to concentrate on my walk with the Lord *right now* instead of getting caught up in where I want to be in my spiritual journey one day.

Loving the Lord at this time of your life, whatever time that may be is an act of worship. You can't bring back yesterday. You're not assured of tomorrow. You only hold this moment of time in your possession.

- What are your feelings about *this time* of your life?

- How can you glorify God in the *now* of your life?

CHAPTER TWENTY-TWO

Age and Body Image

"Stop being perpetually uneasy (anxious and worried)
about your life, what you shall eat or what you shall
drink; or about your body, what you shall put on. Is not
life greater (in quality) than food, and the body
(far above and more excellent) than clothing?"

Matthew 6:25 AMP

There seems to be a direct correlation between the way we feel about our bodies and our self-esteem. Putting proper emphasis on taking care of our bodies is important. Notice I used the word *proper.* If we neglect our bodies as we journey through life, we'll suffer some real and negative physical consequences. But overindulging in things like exercise or dieting is not beneficial either.

The clothing we wear also contributes to our overall body image. This area can easily get out of balance as well. Do you get caught up in the latest styles, splurging on fashion trends, or are you more practical in your approach to what your wear?

I believe "perpetually uneasy" in the Matthew 6:25 verse means placing the focus where Jesus does not want it to be. In other words, it's a good thing to think about what we eat, drink, wear, and how we exercise. But Scripture tells us we should never become obsessed with those things.

I believe it's important to the Lord that we take care of our bodies. By exercising, eating nutritious meals, practicing good physical hygiene, and dressing appropriately, we have opportunity to glorify the one who gave us life and dwells inside our earthly tent.

> *Do you not know that your body is a sanctuary of the Holy Spirit who is in you, whom you have from God? You are not your own, for you were bought at a price; therefore glorify God in your body.*
> (1 Cor. 6:19–20)

I enjoy exercise—well mostly, the benefits of exercise. But years ago I realized that I was overindulging in a good thing. I became preoccupied with running and weight training. Beginning with a healthy focus, I gradually placed too much emphasis on those activities. At some point, I crossed the balance line and was sprinting and toning my way to fatigue and obsession. Thankfully, I saw the warning signs and began to slack off this rigorous training program. Too much is just as unhealthy as too little.

There are many variables contributing to your overall body image. Whatever your age, there's a specific body maintenance program just for you. Doing your best to take care of your body will please the Lord. Think of it as a praise offering to him, taking care of what he has given you. Remembering that the Holy Spirit resides in my body gives me added incentive to keep it in good shape. I so long to honor him by taking care of his dwelling place!

Your body also houses your mind and emotions. We need to be emotionally and mentally healthy and alert, as well as physically so. Here are some strategies to help you find balance in your body image as you age.

- Identify things you like about yourself that have nothing to do with your body. Maybe you have a great sense of humor or you're a great organizer or hostess. Build on those qualities as you begin to take greater care of the physical you.

- Explore your emotions by writing about them in your journal. Focus on growing your positive attitude and ditching some emotions that are weighing you down, like worry or guilt.

- When you look in the mirror, think of something *nice*. Just as you are eager to compliment others on their appearance, find something you like about *you*.

- Take stock of your exercise program. *No exercise program?* Begin one! Exercise is not only good for the body, it's good for the soul! Find something you like to do. Begin a program with a friend. Be creative about it. You can find ways to exercise— even during the busiest days—if you put your mind to it. Think of the time of day you would be most likely to stick to a program. If you hate mornings, then get some exercise at lunch or early in the evening. Many experts agree that twenty minutes of exercise four times a week is a good start. The discipline you build in this area will help you accomplish goals in other areas of your life too!

- It's *your* decision. Be careful about taking the advice of everybody else. This is about you. Don't fall prey to well-meaning people who think they know what you should eat and how you should exercise or look. You know your own body better than anyone else.

And remember, your heavenly Father is interested in every aspect of your life. He created your body, your mind, and gave you emotions and desires that are unique to you. He knows what areas need some extra attention. Ask him to guide you. Let him direct your feelings about your body and give you his take on the best exercise and eating lifestyle for you.

Ask him to brighten your outlook about who you are and his purpose for you. He longs to answer you when you seek his help. Just like a parent is interested in a child, your heavenly Father is interested in *everything* concerning you!

- Glorifying God in your body is a commandment from Scripture. Think about needed changes in your lifestyle that will help you honor him in a greater way.

- You are God's specially designed creation. There's none other like you. Spend some moments thanking God for his design in you. Ask him to help you give the entirety of your body, mind, and spirit to him—following his ways and glorifying him in each area.

CHAPTER TWENTY-THREE

Age and Attitude

But You, LORD, are a shield around me, my glory,
and the One who lifts up my head.

Psalm 3:3

Grandma Pearl lived up to her name. At age ninety-seven, she was indeed a rare and precious find, and continually delighted me with her commitment to a positive attitude. Months ago I walked into White Oak Manor where she lived *and* led the daily exercise program for the residents. The tables and chairs in the dining room were pushed aside, making it a workout floor for the next twenty minutes. With participants in a circle and my grandmom up front, the wheelchair aerobics began. I watched intently as everyone in that circle tried to exercise. I could see the commitment on their faces as they struggled to lift their arms and swing their legs. My grandmom was the perfect instructor, coaching each one to try her best and lift her limbs to whatever degree was comfortable. Their eyes danced as they "swam in the ocean and tiptoed down the beach." Being the cheerleader on the sidelines, I was completely captivated by what was taking place before me. Everything in me applauded as I scanned the faces of those dear ladies who were giving their all to perform each movement. When the routine was finally over, there was great celebration in that room. As they all sat back and relaxed, there was lots of laughter and sighs of victory. It all ended with my grandmom wrapping her arms tightly around herself and calling her comrades to do the same, saying, "Give yourself a big hug—you've done a great thing!"

Attitude has everything to do with your disposition—no matter your age! There are people like my grandmom, who are well along in their years, with wonderful attitudes, while some much younger are prone to gripe and complain. Take a look around you and find women who are growing their positive attitudes, and learn from them. We have an opportunity at whatever age to choose to be positive and live the best we can live during each season of life.

Now let's take a look at a biblical example of a *young* woman who modeled a positive attitude, boldly stepping forth because of her faith in God. She proved to be very useful to the Lord, even at a young age. Pharaoh had commanded that every boy born to the Hebrews be thrown into the Nile, but young Miriam, the sister of Moses, had been trained in the qualities of boldness, wisdom, and courage. In a timely act of faith, she stepped forward to Pharaoh's daughter and asked the question that led to saving the life of Moses and the ultimate delivery of God's chosen people.

> *Now a man from the family of Levi married a Levite woman. The woman became pregnant and gave birth to a son; when she saw that he was beautiful, she hid him for three months. But when she could no longer hide him, she got a papyrus basket for him and coated it with asphalt and pitch. She placed the child in it and set it among the reeds by the bank of the Nile.*

*Then his sister stood at a distance in order to see what
would happen to him. Pharaoh's daughter went down
to bathe at the Nile while her servant girls walked
along the riverbank. Seeing the basket among the
reeds, she sent her slave girl to get it. When she opened
it, she saw the child—a little boy, crying. She felt sorry
for him and said, "This is one of the Hebrew boys."*

*Then his sister said to Pharaoh's daughter,
"Should I go and call a woman from the Hebrews to
nurse the boy for you?"*

*"Go," Pharaoh's daughter told her. So the girl
went and called the boy's mother.* (Exod. 2:1–8)

Miriam's attitude of faith enabled her to act courageously and intervene as God's ambassador for the Hebrew
race.

In every age of life, we have opportunity to serve our
heavenly Father! His calling on our lives is not reserved for
only a particular span of our lifetime. We have opportunity
to glorify him—whatever our age!

I thank the Lord for the women of all ages who are
attending Frazzled Female events and going through the
Bible studies. One commonality we all share is that no
matter our age, each of us is getting older!

Most of the time, getting older is just fine with me.
Truthfully speaking, however, there are other times when
I seem to have difficulty getting over the fact that I'm get-
ting older.

Here are some promises of Scripture that are meaning-
ful to me when I'm less than excited about moving on up
the time line of life! Perhaps they'll be comforting to you,
as well.

- He planned out every single day of your life before
  you were born!

*Your eyes saw me when I was formless; all my
days were written in Your book and planned before a
single one of them began.* (Ps. 139:16)

- He is never closer to you than he is at this very
  moment!

  *I will be the same until your old age, and I will
  bear you up when you turn gray. I have made you,
  and I will carry you; I will bear and save you.*
  (Isa. 46:4)

- Your body will change. Your appearance will
  change. Your Jesus will never change!

  *Jesus Christ is the same yesterday and today and
  forever.* (Heb. 13:8 NIV)

- Is your attitude glorifying to God?

- This time of your life is special to your God. What
  are some changes you can make to grow a more
  positive attitude?

CHAPTER TWENTY-FOUR

Embracing the Moment

> He restores my soul. He guides me in paths
> of righteousness for his name's sake.
>
> **Psalm 23:3** NIV

Some of you have heard about it and have it to look forward to. Others have weathered it and gotten to the other side. Many of you are in the throes of it now! I'm talking about that middle time of life that ushers in all sorts of new feelings, shaky expectations, and possible opportunities. I heard about it long before I got here, and I'll be sharing about it long after I leave. Everybody I know has (or will have) a midlife crisis story. Here's what's going on with my forty-five-year-old friend, Pat:

With her third daughter now in college, Pat has shifted her focus—from soccer games, proms, and late-night vigils—to exercise and competition. She's embracing this new time of life as an opportunity to take better care of herself and improve her health. She's also enjoying the rush of running in races and accomplishing goals she never even thought of attacking before. With a twinkle in her eye, she tells me, "It's just my midlife crisis!"

Jesus said in Matthew 7:17, "Every good tree bears good fruit, but a bad tree bears bad fruit" (NIV).

I notice that the age of the tree is not mentioned. You know why? It doesn't matter! You can "bear good fruit" when you're young, when you're old, and when you're in-between!

Sometimes I hear people make excuses because of age, as if the infirmities that happen along the time line of life give us excuses not to bear good fruit. That's simply not biblical. I fully believe that if you're a Christian, it is God's design for you to bear fruit at every age of life. True, there may be limitations of being too young, too old, or too inexperienced. But you see, we are not called to bear *all* the good fruit—just some of it. *And the good fruit we are to bear is the good fruit he is calling us to bear.*

Along with the age comment, I've heard many women use hormones for an excuse, along with aches and pains that give way to griping and complaining because of age-related illnesses. Well, I've come to a conclusion: Old crabby women were young crabby women. You're not crabby because you're old. You're crabby because you're crabby!

I'm not intending to pass judgment or be critical of anyone who suffers through pain-filled days and stressed-out emotions. I'm just saying (and through the love of Jesus) that you need to take a look at "where you are" right now. Are you using conditions in your life to keep you from experiencing his love and bearing his fruit? My ninety-seven-year-old grandmother who faithfully led the exercise program in her nursing home could have very easily used aches, pains, and the inability to walk as an excuse not to lead in exercise. And if she did, nobody would blame her. But since she didn't, many women experienced a special blessing for their bodies and their spirits.

It's easy and tempting to get dragged down by those age-related physical pains. In fact, aging can be downright depressing! Any amens? If you approach getting older from a worldly view, you can very easily sink on down in despair as those years creep on and pile up.

But there's good news, and it is indeed good! It's also freeing and exciting. With Jesus Christ living in your heart, you can face each and every day with fresh excitement because he becomes your excitement for living. He will give you energy for each new day and a new passion for each new stage of life. You truly can embrace life, just like my friend Pat, with new and constructive energy to live life in a different way. Physically, emotionally, and mentally, you're apt to have to adapt, but you can do this—and enjoy the journey—if you put Christ first. He is interested in your physical body, your emotional chemistry, and your mental clarity, and he *will* restore the joy to living if you lean on him during each phase of it!

> *The rain came down, the streams rose, and the winds blew and beat against that house; yet it did not fall, because it had its foundation on the rock.* (Matt. 7:25 NIV)

The reality is, dear friend, unless Jesus lives in your heart and rules your mind and emotions, your "house" will shatter to pieces. Each stage of life presents new and potentially destructive challenges. At each stage of my life there have been difficult physical, emotional, and mental challenges. Life's just like that. Had I not been clinging to the rock, I would be much more battered and bruised than I am today.

I've become a woman on a mission! I'm determined to no longer make excuses because of limitations of my age. I'm continuing to build on that holy foundation, and

I'm going to bear good fruit for Jesus with a smile on my face and a song in my heart. And maybe one day, if I keep at it, my grandmom—with a smile of encouragement and a twinkle in her eye—will toss over her baton!

- What excuses have you made for not bearing *good fruit* for Jesus?

- If getting older has rattled you a bit, welcome to the club! It's time for you to sink into the love of God and allow him to redefine your focus for living. What can you do, starting now, to help you be more positive as you age?

CHAPTER TWENTY-FIVE

Life to the Fullest

"I know the plans I have for you," declares the
LORD, "plans to prosper you and not to harm you,
plans to give you hope and a future."

Jeremiah 29:11 NIV

I've often heard my friend Janet remark, "I want to be a ballerina when I grow up!" I smile every time I hear her say it. She is a school principal and close to getting her doctorate in administration. She loves her work and is quite content in it. And yet, there's a longing somewhere deep down to have a simpler lifestyle—one that embraces the joy of living and self-expression.

Do you ever have those feelings? Is there someone you'd like to be that you never got to be? Is there something you'd like to do that you never got to do?

One of the definitions of *maturing* is "becoming fully developed and perfected." That's how I like to think of growing older. It sounds more noble and even classy to realize I'm developing and moving toward perfection instead of getting old!

Paul hit it right when he said:

> *Not that I have already obtained all this, or*
> *have already been made perfect, but I press on to take*
> *hold of that for which Christ Jesus took hold of me.*
> *Brothers [sisters!], I do not consider myself yet to have*
> *taken hold of it. But one thing I do: Forgetting what*
> *is behind and straining toward what is ahead, I press*
> *on toward the goal to win the prize . . . All of us who*
> *are mature should take such a view of things.*
> (Phil. 3:12–15 NIV)

Part of this "moving toward perfection" is letting go of past regrets. Whether it's regretting things done or things left undone, there's simply no reason to hang on to them. You have no opportunity to relive and redo yesterday's moments, but you do have every opportunity to do it right now. Those scars of the past can be very useful.

Five years ago I had neck surgery that left a three-inch scar on my throat. I tried every ointment and miracle cream I could find and still could not make it disappear. As months and years have passed, it faded but remained visible. Gradually I made peace with that ol' scar. Instead of looking at it now with disgust, I see it as a reminder of a time when God truly helped me keep my sanity in the midst of physical pain!

Scars come physically, emotionally, and mentally. Sometimes they are the result of our own etching. Other times they come as the result of hurt inflicted by others. Regardless of the reason the scars are there, God can change your view of them. And he's the *only* one who can transform your feelings of disgust and despair into peace and joy. He alone can deliver you from the past so you can relax and enjoy the present!

The following guidelines can help release you from yesterday's scars and reset your focus on Christ's love—so you can live life to the fullest!

- *Recognize your need for God.* We get in trouble when we try to make it on our own. Women are notorious for that. We aim toward perfection in family relationships, business endeavors, and volunteer work. We even become compulsive about our hobbies or friends. Now is a good time for you to back off! Tell your heavenly Father you need him more than you need anybody else. And you need a relationship with him more than you need to do things for him. Talk with him about it. Realize the joy of the NOW, in his presence.

- *Refuse to compare yourself with others.* Looking at other women who seem to have it all together is a real temptation. You may have an unhealthy ambition of trying to be like someone else. God has a unique plan for you. His purpose for each of his children is God-designed, and only he knows what that plan is. Spend time in his Word and expect him to speak to you about who you are in him. Rediscover your true identity!

- *Develop godly relationships.* One of the most wonderfully beneficial and joyful things I've done as I've "matured" through the years is to latch on to a few close buddies. There's *strength in numbers,* you know. When you age with a friend, you can compare notes and spur each other on. To know my friend has experienced the same struggles I face as I age is so encouraging. These friendships are truly a gift from Jesus!

- *Try something new.* Honestly, it wouldn't surprise me if my friend Janet dons her ballerina shoes and joyfully twirls around—well, for a short while at least. She loves Jesus and she's learned that life

is full of new experiences just *waiting to be had*.
Trying new things gives you energy and a zest
for living—not to mention the laughs! I love to
have a good time, and some of my most joyful life
experiences come from doing things just for the
enjoyment of doing them.

So forge ahead, dear sister! Life's coming at you, and
it's coming fast. It's your choice to embrace each moment
of each day—whatever your age—in the joy and exuber-
ance of Jesus!

- What is something you've never done before but
  have always wanted to do?

- Is it safe, legal, and fun?

Go for it!

Victoriously Frazzled!

There is a river—its streams delight the city of God,
the holy dwelling place of the Most High.
God is within her; she will not be toppled.
God will help her when the morning dawns.

Psalm 46:4–5

*I*t was early morning and I was meeting my friend Ginger
for breakfast to celebrate her birthday.

During my normal time of life, I loved early! Oh yes.
Early was a thriving time for me. There was plenty of time
for quiet moments with Jesus, and then I'd get moving
on whatever projects were before me that day. I've always
loved the freshness, the new beginnings, and even the
smell of morning. Until . . .

I stumbled—along with every other female baby
boomer I know—into the land of hot flashes and sleepless
nights! Gone were the days of being only mildly interested
in the symptoms tons of women around me were going
through. Now it was *me* and I became a woman on a mission to find the answer to *How the smack do you deal with
this?*

Breakfast with my dear friend was a good place to start.
She just poured out empathy as I presented all my discom-
forts and frustrations. I was beginning to feel a little better

just from baring my soul, when my flailing arms—in one fell swoop—took out a waitress (and her tray of entrees) who got in my path while heading to a corner table of now frustrated and hungrier than ever early risers.

"Oh my" from Ginger, and "ahhhhh" from fifty onlookers, and a hundred unspoken words from the glare of the waitress slit my already frayed emotions. After ten seconds of shocked suspension, I reacted the way any all-together, in-control, dependent-upon-God woman would. I burst into tears!

Whether it was the intensity of the moment or the daggers in the eyes of the waitress that caused my outburst, I knew I was a goner. I'd used the last of my positive emotional reserves to make it out of the house that morning, leaving absolutely nothing to deal with this kind of unexpected turmoil.

Ginger, with tears of "I'm with ya, honey," looked with steel eyes into mine and said, "It didn't happen."

I blubbered, "Huh?"

"It didn't happen," she said. "That's what my coach would tell me when I'd mess up during our softball games. He'd say, 'For the benefit of the whole team, you have to convince yourself it never happened. If you don't, you'll be focusing on that mistake for the rest of the game, and we will all suffer.'"

In view of the eggs and bacon splattered around my feet, I knew this would prove to be quite a challenge. Hours later, reflecting on the mishap and what my friend had said, God touched me with his truth. The whole messed-up scene of the eggs and bacon spiraling to the floor and Ginger's comment of "It didn't happen" painted the very picture of the atoning sacrifice of Jesus. Now I truly believe that God gives us "pictures" every day of his undying love for us, and for me it became crystal clear once again from those few seconds of chaos. He longs to show us throughout daily living—good times, bad times—the true essence of his love. Because of him, all of our mess ups have been canceled, and we can live victoriously each and every moment of every day!

Even in the middle of turmoil, his truth rings loud and clear! He is in control—even when it doesn't appear so.

You see, it's easy to see God in the powerful and extraordinary ways he manifests his presence, but you have to grow the discipline of seeing him in the bacon and eggs on the floor. But he was there that day, loving me and assuring me as I tried to regain my composure. I'm beginning to discover his divine design anywhere and everywhere, and I'm telling you—there's no greater way to live!

God created us so that we could know him and grow a relationship with him. He longs for us to spend time with him so that he can reveal to us who he is. In order to transform our minds and lift our thinking above *ordinary worldly attitudes,* we must spend time studying his word, meditating and talking with him as we go.

We are commanded in Scripture to love him whole-heartedly.

> *Love the Lord your God with all your heart, with all your soul, and with all your strength.* (Deut. 6:5)

As we love him, we spend time with him. As we spend time with him, we take on his thoughts. Then we start to lose some things: anger, guilt, anxiety, frustration, critical attitudes, worry, along with other energy-draining negative thinking. It's a holy progression that leads us to become more confident as we model his love and share it with others.

While talking with Martha, who was irritated that her sister Mary was not helping out, Jesus comments:

> *Mary has chosen the good portion (that which*
> *is to her advantage), which shall not be taken away*
> *from her.* (Luke 10:42 AMP)

For years now, my heart has been hungry to find out more about these *advantages* lavished upon me as I grow deep into the love of Jesus. These blessings are priceless, and Jesus says they'll never be taken away!

The advantages realized in a deep and intimate relationship with Jesus Christ will help us realize that heaven is our true home. And though the world may collapse around us, our God is strong and victorious within us!

This little book is all about our victorious Savior, who offers victorious living to each of us who choose to spend time with him and learn his ways. It is my prayer that you will take the message to heart. The love that my Father has given me in ministering to women through speaking and writing has fueled a deep desire to honor him in everything I say and everything I write.

It's my prayer that you'll fall in love with Jesus as you spend time getting to know him through his Word. I pray that you'll long to worship him in singing, dancing, journaling, walking, and just breathing in his glory. I pray that you'll see him in the exceptional things of life, as well as those unpredicted chaotic moments that fill much of your days.

And more than anything, I pray that you'll know that you know that you know—he's covered every guilt, shame, every sin through the blood of the cross. Because of his sacrificial death, it's as if *it never happened!*

Are you beginning to be filled with a new longing to thank him? Fall in love with him—deeper than you've ever been before. To know him is to love him, and to love him is to long to know him more and more. It's a *victorious journey!*

Going Deeper

•   If you've never had a consistent quiet time with
Jesus, begin by setting aside ten minutes in the early
morning. Keep at it, consistently keeping your divine
appointment. Do this for one month, and gradually
increase your time with the Lord. The Holy Spirit will
lead you in the amount of time that's just right for you at
this stage of your life. Reviewing chapter 20 will help you
get started.

•   Want to love God more? Realize his deep love for
you. Take some time to journal notes to Jesus. Talk to
him in your writing, as you would a friend. Write about
things and people you're thankful for, listing them. Tell
him why you're thankful. Every day there are ways God
reveals his love to you. Write about some of these. Keep
this journal for two weeks. Write at lunch, or on break, or
before going to bed. At the end of two weeks, go back and
review with a heart full of gratitude.

•   Take a fast on negative thinking. Every time a
negative thought comes into your mind, shoot it out and
replace it with Scripture. Here's one I use: *This is the day
the* LORD *has made. I will rejoice and be glad in it!*
(see Ps. 118:24).

•   There's power in praise! Set aside a ten-minute
praise session each day for one week. This can be
anytime, anywhere. Vary your praise offerings. You might
sing, or write, or dance, or draw, etc. Be creative in your
praise. There's not a set way to praise God. Let your
praise flow from a heart full of love. Write about your
experience in your journal at the end of the week.

Advantages of Growing Deeper in Love with Jesus

•   **Fulfillment.** As you spend time getting to know Jesus by going to that quiet place with him, your joy will increase. There's nothing on Earth as sweet or as satisfying as growing your love relationship with your Savior. You will progressively become aware of his closeness to you throughout your day.

> *Shout for joy, you heavens! Earth, rejoice! Mountains break into joyful shouts! For the LORD has comforted His people, and will have compassion on His afflicted ones.* (Isa. 49:13)

•   **Transformed mind.** When difficulties of life happen, you'll be calmer and able to think more clearly. Your human nature, which acts in a reactionary way, will fade into the background as the supernatural power of Jesus takes over. Anger, resentment, and criticism will be replaced with a gentler spirit.

> *And the peace of God, which surpasses every thought, will guard your hearts and your minds in Christ Jesus.* (Phil. 4:7)

•   **Soothed nerves.** Instead of insisting on "your way," you'll rest in the assurance that God will provide in his way and in his timing. Trusting in him will be more likely because you've spent time with him.

> *The LORD is good, a refuge in times of trouble. He cares for those who trust in him.* (Nahum 1:7 NIV)

• **Divine direction.** When you consistently spend time with Jesus, getting to know him and recognizing his voice, you'll be more in tune with him throughout your daily activities. You'll learn to lean on him more, asking his spirit to help you make decisions. You'll ask for his help in doing the daily kinds of things that you do. It will become normal to seek and receive his direction.

> *Let me experience Your faithful love in the morning, for I trust in You. Reveal to me the way I should go, because I long for You.* (Ps. 143:8)

• **A life that brings glory to God.** The world's ways are so different from God's. When you spend time with Jesus, people will notice. You'll exhibit his characteristics of peace, joy, excitement, faith, and steadfastness when others are reacting in worldly ways. And how glorifying—when they see Jesus in you!

> *Be completely humble and gentle; be patient, bearing with one another in love. Make every effort to keep the unity of the Spirit through the bond of peace.* (Eph. 4:2–3 NIV)

How to Become a Christian

God wants us to love him above anyone or anything else because loving him puts everything else in life in perspective. In God we find the hope, peace, and joy that are possible only through a personal relationship with him. Through his presence in our lives, we can truly love one another because God is love. John 3:16 says, "For God loved the world in this way: He gave His One and Only Son, so that everyone who believes in Him will not perish but have eternal life."

In order to live an abundant life, we must accept God's gift of love. "I have come that they may have life and have it in abundance" (John 10:10).

A relationship with God begins by admitting we are not perfect. We continue to fall short of God's standards. Romans 3:23 says, "For all have sinned and fall short of the glory of God."

The price for these wrong doings is separation from God. "For the wages of sin is death, but the gift of God is eternal life in Christ Jesus our Lord" (Rom. 6:23).

God's love comes to us right in the middle of our sin. "But God proves His own love for us in that while we were still sinners Christ died for us!" (Rom. 5:8).

He doesn't ask us to clean up our lives first. In fact, without his help we are incapable of living by his standards.

Forgiveness begins when we admit our sin to God. When we do, he is faithful to forgive and restore our relationship with him. "If we confess our sins, He is faithful and righteous to forgive us our sins and to cleanse us from all unrighteousness" (1 John 1:9).

Scripture confirms that this love gift and relationship with God are not just for a special few but for everyone. "For everyone who calls on the name of the Lord will be saved" (Rom. 10:13).

If you would like to receive God's gift of salvation, pray this prayer:

> *Dear God, I know that I am imperfect and separated from you. Please forgive me for my sin and adopt me as your child. Thank you for this gift of life through the sacrifice of your Son. I believe Jesus died for my sins. I will live my life for you. Amen.*

If you prayed this prayer for the first time, share with someone! Talk to a pastor or Christian friend. To grow in your Christian walk, continue to cultivate your love for Jesus through Scripture study and fellowship with other Christians.

Welcome to God's family!

Notes

1. John and Stasi Eldredge, *Captivating* (Nashville, TN: Nelson Books, 2005), 28.

2. Oswald Chambers, *My Utmost for His Highest* (Grand Rapids, MI: Discovery House Publishers, 1992), January 26.

3. Ibid., October 30.

4. Billy Graham, *The Holy Spirit* (Dallas, London, Vancouver, Melbourne: W Publishing Group), 127.

5. Ibid.

6. Wesley and Stacey Campbell, *Praying the Bible* (Ventura, CA: Regal from Gospel Light, 2002), 34.